NINETEENTH-CENTURY
BRITISH PHILOSOPHY

THOEMMES
REPRINTS

AN
ANALYSIS
OF
KANT'S
CRITICK OF PURE REASON

Francis Haywood

THOEMMES
BRISTOL

© 1990 Thoemmes Antiquarian Books Ltd

Published by
Thoemmes Antiquarian Books Ltd
85 Park Street
Bristol BS1 5PJ

ISBN 1 85506 031 0

This is a reprint of the 1844 Edition

Publisher's Note

ANALYSIS OF KANT'S CRITICK

OF PURE REASON.

AN ANALYSIS OF KANT'S CRITICK

OF PURE REASON

BY THE

TRANSLATOR OF THAT WORK

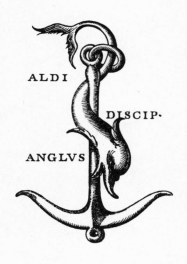

ALDI
DISCIP.
ANGLVS

LONDON
WILLIAM PICKERING
1844

PREFACE.

THE following Epitome of the " Critick of Pure Reason," has been undertaken to elucidate those points, which, notwithstanding a translation, made about three years ago, of the work itself still remain unintelligible. Whether this may be the fault of the original work, or of the ineffectual attempt to render it into English, is not to be discussed. The language of the author seems to be frequently so obscure as certainly to throw great obstacles in the way of a right comprehension of the subject. Whether man is purely a material agent, or whether the instruments only through which he works are material, is of all considerations the most important, and it is because the distinction has been pointed out by Kant in a manner which seems to solve the question that his writings are of such universal interest. The present analysis is founded upon and couched in the words of the original work : for though different great commentators have been more or less closely followed, yet, as they themselves have in most cases borrowed their phraseology

from Kant himself, they are not so entirely
copied in this analysis as, in looking merely at
the expressions used, might seem to be the case.
In several instances, however, not only their
mode of reasoning, but their form of language,
has been implicitly adopted, and from Wirg-
man in particular, as well as from Schœn, and
Beck, and from Jouffroy's translation of a
German Analysis, much that is in the following
work will be found to have been taken.   The object of the author or compiler was less origi-
nality, than to render his subject comprehensible; and, if this be attained, the end he had
in view will be fully accomplished, and for this
he is willing to forego any higher claim of
authorship.

KANTIAN PRINCIPLES,

OR THE ANALYSIS OF

"THE CRITICK OF PURE REASON."

PREFACE.

In 1781, Kant published his first edition of this celebrated work, the preface to which is short, and hardly does more than introduce the subject generally ; but in 1790, together with a second edition a second preface appeared, wherein the leading principles of the system are set forth. The exposition commences by showing that Logic, unlike the cognition of Reason, is a science which from the earliest times has proceeded in a right path, and that even so soon as the days of Aristotle this was discovered ; and that though the subject may not have made great advances since that period, it has not retrograded.

If psychological, metaphysical, or anthropological elements have been incorrectly pushed into Logic, this, it is contended, though it may have disfigured the science,—inasmuch as it added considerations which do not properly appertain to it,— was a mistake, rather than a fault. Logic in Kant's view of the matter has, in fact, nothing to do but

with the formal rules of all thinking, whether such
be à priori, or empirical.

Logic then being limited in this way, the Understanding therein is only concerned with itself and
its form. Reason, the particular subject-matter
of Kant's investigation, is twofold, theoretical or
practical, and its cognitions may be so referred to its
object. But, in the present instance, the pure part
of both is only to be treated, that is to say, that
part wherein reason determines its object wholly
à priori ; and that which proceeds from other sources
must not be mixed up with it.

Mathematics and Physics are adduced as the
two theoretical cognitions of Reason which have to
determine their objects à priori, the first of which is
stated to have always proceeded in a right track
from the earliest period of Greece ; it had, however,
more difficulty in getting into this proper way than
Logic, where, as it was before said, the understanding or reason has only to do with itself. With
Physics, again, this was more difficult, and it was
not until the time of Galileo that a light is supposed
to have dawned upon natural philosophers. It was
then discovered that reason only perceives that
which it itself produces, and that its judgments coincide with certain laws existing in the understanding. Reason, in this way, though it refers to nature,
in order to be instructed by it, experimentally, yet
in fact itself gives laws to nature, compelling the
answers to be rendered in certain forms.

This is the essence of the system of Kant, and
upon which every thing depends ; and though it
seems something like the exploded doctrine of innate
ideas, yet it will be ascertained in the sequel to be
very different.

Metaphysics not having, like Mathematics, the advantage of Intuition, have been longer in falling into the sure path of a science ; for reason comes to a stand-still, when it wishes to discover, à priori, laws which, it insists, the most common experience confirms. The error in metaphysical speculations seems to have been, that it has hitherto been laid down, that our cognition was to regulate itself according to the objects, whilst, under such a supposition, all attempts to make out anything, à priori, respecting these objects, by means of conceptions, whereby our cognition would be extended, have failed. The next thing then to be tried is whether it would not be better to admit that the objects are regulated according to our cognition. This accords more with the possibility that is desired of their cognition à priori, which is to determine something respecting them before they are given.

Copernicus, it is known, made little progress in his knowledge of the motions of the heavenly bodies so long as he supposed that the stars revolved round the spectator, but when he reversed the idea, and made the spectator to turn and the sun itself to be at rest, he arrived at the true result. All objects according to this improved mode of thinking regulate themselves as objects of experience, in which character alone they are known, according to cognitions à priori, existing in the understanding. The contradictions that arise in our investigations of reason, flow from confounding the objects that are presented to us in one case as Objects of experience, and in another as Things in themselves.

This is the great distinction of the Kantian System. Reason, for instance, aspires to the Unconditioned. But if we admit our cognition of experience regulates itself according to objects, as Things in themselves, the unconditioned cannot be thought without contradiction ; whilst if we suppose that our representation of things as they are given to us, does not regulate itself according to these, as things in themselves, but that these objects, as phenomena, rather regulate themselves according to our mode of representation, the contradiction disappears. The analysis of pure cognition à priori by the metaphysician is or ought to be divided into the two classes mentioned, namely, that of Things in themselves, and Things as phenomena. Carrying the experience-view of things out to its strict consequences, it would seem to exalt Sensibility or Sensation high above all other principles, but this Kant is peculiarly anxious to avoid ; and by endeavouring to show that the practical or moral use of Reason is no less true and demonstrable than the speculative, and in having cleared the way of all that was obstructive, he thinks he affords freer passage to the dictates of the moral principle. The Critick of Pure Reason limits the use of reason, in this way, that it admits Space and Time to be merely Forms of sensible intuition, consequently only the conditions of things as phenomena ; and it further shows, that we can have no elements at all for the cognition of things, excepting so far as a corresponding intuition can be given to these conceptions—consequently, that we can have no cognition of an object, as a thing in itself, but merely so far as it is an object of sensible intuition, that is, so far as it is Phenomenon.

The analytical part of the Critick of Pure Reason is devoted to the proof of these assertions, and restrains thereby the speculative cognition of Reason, as has been remarked, to mere objects of experi-

ence. But then there arises the greatest difference
between cognizing or knowing objects, and thinking
them ; and the antagonist views which Kant afterwards developes in what he terms Antinomies, are
only to be explained by admitting two modes of
contemplating the objects, namely, in the one case,
to look upon things, as things in themselves, and in
the other, as they are phenomenal, or as they appear. Kant intimates, that through his view of the
case, and the great distinction which he establishes,
the doctrines of Materialism and Atheism are totally uprooted, and he insists that the outcry raised
against his system arises not from the public, who
are never injured by any speculative opinion, but
from schoolmen, who alone are interested in main-
taining their selfish and prejudiced positions.

Thus ends the preface to the Critick of Pure Reason : and the reasoning by which these principles
are to be supported forms the subject of a work
which, however disfigured by a harsh and singular
terminology, must always be regarded as one of the
most important productions connected with the
history of the human mind.

The Introduction to the work itself of the Critick
of Pure Reason begins by exposing the difference
between pure and empirical cognition or knowledge ; and whilst it admits that this said cognition
begins with experience, it denies that it springs
up out of experience—empirical cognition being a
compound of that which we have received through
our impressions ; and that which our own inherent,
as it may be termed, cognition-faculty, (called
however only into action by impressions made upon
the senses) has supplied from or out of itself.

Hence, according to this view, although all knowledge commences its operations from experience,
which is designated variously as sensible, sensual,
or sensitive, the one does not flow from the other ;
the very facts of experience being conceived and
arranged according to innate forms of the understanding, and which are subsequently shown to be
so many Categories of Pure Reason. Cognitions
à priori are such as are entirely independent of
experience, though by this experience alone are
they called into operation ; and Cognitions, à posteriori, are, on the other hand, those which have
their source in experience. Pure knowledge, à
priori, is that with which nothing at all empirical is
mixed, so that the proposition that " every change
has its cause," notwithstanding that it is a proposition à priori, is not pure ; because change is a
conception which can only be derived from experience. In the same way it is erroneous, in speaking of one who undermines the foundation of his
house, to say that he might, à priori, have known
the house would fall ; because this entirely, à priori,
he could not be acquainted with, for heaviness is in
this case added ; and that bodies themselves are
heavy, and that they fall when their supports are
taken away, is a species of knowledge only derivable from experience.

It being admitted that the human mind is always
in possession of certain cognitions à priori, the only
question then is, what is the criterion by which such
are distinguished from those that are à posteriori ?
This criterion is Necessity and strict Universality,
and wherever either of these belong to a Judgment,
they are such characteristics as indicate a peculiar
source of cognition, or the one which is à priori.

Experience can only give contingent judgments; and Hume's idea of the necessary connexion of Cause and Effect being simply in our minds the result of Habit, is precisely the doctrine which Kant opposes, and to which the world is indebted for the publication of the Critick of Pure Reason.

Now if what has been stated as to cognitions à priori be true, the necessity of a science which should establish positively the principles and extent of the same is obvious, and the most important of all these to man are the questions of God, Liberty, and Immortality, and the Critick of Pure Reason is the essential preliminary to that of Practical Reason, wherein these three points are to be fully proved and determined. To prepare the way for this investigation, it will be first necessary to shew the difference that exists between the different kinds of Judgments, or those which are analytical and synthetical.

A Judgment is called analytical, when the predicate adds nothing to the conception of the subject, but only by analysis separates it into its constituent parts. This is merely an explicative judgment, but a synthetical one is an extending or amplifying judgment; inasmuch as it adds a predicate to the conception of the subject, which was not at all thought in it, and could not by any analysis of the same have been added to it. Thus mathematical judgments are all synthetical, and mathematical propositions are judgments à priori, and not empirical, because they carry along with them the test of necessity, which it is evident is not derivable from experience.

The questions then arise, how these synthetical judgments à priori, are possible, as well as how pure Mathematics, and pure Physics are possible ; but these sciences being taken for granted, the transition takes place to Metaphysics, and the question is then asked also as to possibility in this case, and this again leads to the idea and division of a particular science, to be denominated by the title of the Critick of Pure Reason.

Here the objects and limits of the work itself are determined. It is not to be designated Transcendental Philosophy, because, to be a complete system in this sense, it ought to contain a full analysis of the whole of human cognition à priori ; but whilst " the Critick " as a work lays before us a complete enumeration of all the fundamental conceptions of the human mind, or of the categories which form the aforesaid pure cognition, it refrains from a full analysis of these conceptions themselves, as well as from such as are thence derived. Limiting itself thus to the consideration of synthetical cognition à priori, the science is separated into the two great divisions of the Elemental Doctrine, or the Doctrine of the elements of the subject, and the Methodical Doctrine, or that which is to determine the method that is to be applied to these elements.

The interpretation is here to be afforded of what is termed by Kant, Transcendental Æsthetick, or the theory or rules of sensibility in general, and intuition is declared to be the only means by which reference is made to objects, and whereby immediate (as distinct from other) cognition is afforded. To realize this the object must be given to us, and the effect of the object upon the representation-faculty of man is Sensation ; that which corresponds, in the phenomenon, to the sensation is Matter, and that which causes that the diversity of the phenomenon is adduced in certain relationship is Form.

By means of the external sense we represent to ourselves every thing as in Space; and by the internal sense all is represented in the relationship of Time.

But the question arises what are these two things, space and time? Are they determinations or relations of things, but yet such as would belong to these things in themselves, though they should not be intuited or envisaged ; or are they such things that they belong only to the form of the intuition, and consequently to a subjective property of mind, without which these attributes could not be attached to any thing.

After discussing in this way what space is, Kant arrives at the conclusion that space is an intuition à priori, and not a conception. Space in his view is held to be nothing but the form of all phenomena of the external sense, or the subjective condition of sensibility, under which alone external intuition is possible to us ; and it will be seen from considering the doctrine, that the Reality or objective validity of space is positive, in reference to all that, externally, as object, can be presented to us ; but at the same time that it is an Ideality in reference to things if they are considered in themselves, by means of reason or without regard to the nature of our sensibility. Here the distinction shows itself, between things in themselves, and things as they appear. Space is not a form which is proper to things in themselves, nor are such things at all known to us. What we term external objects are nothing but mere representations of our sensibility, whose form is in space, but whose true correlative, that is to say, the thing in itself, is not thereby, nor can it be known.

Neither is Time any empirical conception which can be adduced from experience. It is a necessary representation which lies at the foundation of all intuition. Time is given, à priori :—it is the form of the internal sense, and the formal condition, à priori, of phenomena in general. Hence it will be seen that all intuition is nothing but the representation of phenomena ; that the things we see or envisage are not in themselves what they are taken for ; that if we did away with ourselves, that is to say, the subject or the subjective quality of our senses in general, every quality that we discover in time and space, and even time and space themselves would disappear. What objects may be in themselves, separated from the receptivity of our sensibility is quite unknown to us. We only are acquainted with our own mode of perceiving these objects. The pure intuitions are space and time ; the empirical is sensation. Here the error of the Leibnitzian-Wolfian Philosophy becomes palpable, for in the view there taken of our cognitions, the difference between that which was intellectual and that which appertains to the sensibility was considered merely as logical; whereas it is transcendental, concerning not merely the form as to clearness or obscurity, but the origin and content of our cognitions themselves.

The science, which treats of the laws of the understanding in general is termed Logic, as that which treated of the science of sensibility or sensitivity was Æsthetick. But Logic is divided into two branches accordingly as it signifies the universal or the particular use of the understanding. The one contains the absolutely necessary rules of Thinking in general, the other contains rules as to thinking correctly, in regard to particular kind of objects. The one is Elemental Logic, or general Logic, the other the Organon or understanding-instrument of this or that particular science. Elemental logic is for the most part taught in the schools as propædeutical or preparatory to what is to follow ; though in progress of the development of the human intellect, we only attain to its general principles when we have become acquainted with the objects themselves ; since previous to this, it would be difficult to indicate the rules in respect of the science which particularly attaches to them.

Now this elemental or general Logic may be divided again into two branches, pure and applied. In the one abstraction is made of all the empirical conditions under which the understanding is exercised, as for instance, the influence of the senses, the power of custom, of inclination, desire, passion, the sources of prejudices, &c. ; as well as all causes of experience-cognitions, inasmuch as these merely concern the application of the understanding to sensible impressions. Pure elemental, or universal, or general logic, only regards pure principles, à priori ; and is therefore a canon of the understanding and reason, (or a complex of rules for the faculty of forming conceptions, and judging and concluding), yet it considers the formal part and what, as thinking, is necessarily required for thinking, the content of the same being either empirical, that is, derived from experience, or transcendental, that is to say, concerning cognitions à priori. This elemental or universal logic is termed applied elemental logic when it is directed to the rules of the use of the understanding under alleged subjective empirical - psychological conditions, as for example, when it is directed to the play of the imagination, &c. Still it is universal Logic, though it has empirical principles, for this reason, that it refers to the use of the understanding without distinction of objects, and in this way it becomes neither exactly an Organon (or an understanding - instrument) of particular sciences, (which contains the rules of thinking as to a particular kind of objects,) nor a Canon of the understanding in general, because it contains the application of the use of the understanding to a determinate thinking subject, that is to say, man ; but it is only a Cathartikon, (means of purification) of the common understanding from error.

In elemental Logic the part which is pure, or which regards pure Reason, must be separated from that which constitutes what is applied, though still elemental or universal logic. As a science it appears dry. It is, however, a systematic cognition, though a short one. It derives all its positions from the understanding, and is nothing else but an analysis or development of the functions of the understanding in thinking or in thought generally. Logicians must therefore at all times have the two rules before them in treating of elemental logic ; for when it is considered under the sense of universal, it makes abstraction of the content of all understanding-cognition ; or of all reference of the same to the object ; consequently in respect to the same, whether the cognition be pure or empirical ; whether the object springs from the cognition-faculty itself, or is given by means of sensible impressions. For if it were admitted that it has re-

ference to the difference of objects of thought, then
by reason of this difference, and because the same
is frequently given by experience, it could not assume strict universality, as to its rules, because these
rules might change according to the difference of
objects.   Elemental logic in this way considers
simply the logical form in respect of cognitions one to
another, that is, it has only to do with the pure form
of thought.   But as pure logic it has no empirical
principles, and consequently it derives nothing from
psychology, which has no influence upon the canon
of the understanding.   Pure elemental Logic is a
demonstrated doctrine.   All is entirely in it à priori,
that is, must carry along with it necessity and universality.

Applied Logic is a representation of the necessary
understanding-use under the contingent conditions
of the subject.   It treats of attention, its obstacles
and consequences, the origin of error, &c.   Universal
and pure logic has the same reference to this that
pure morality has to Ethics.

Logic must again be further divided into different parts, and the divisions before given of universal and particular and of pure and applied will
not suffice.   There is besides a transcendental logic.

Universal Logic, as we have observed, makes
abstraction of all content of cognition, that is, reference to its object, or of all relationship to the object, considering only logical form in the relations
of cognitions to each other, or the form of thought
in general.   But as we are aware that there are
pure as well as empirical intuitions,—there is also
a difference between pure and empirical thinking,
and there is likewise a Logic in which we should
not make abstraction of all content of the intuition,

as universal or elemental logic does, which has
nothing to do with difference as to pure or empirical thinking in particular, but with thinking in
general. This other science, or that of conceptions,
à priori, is called transcendental Logic, and it forms
a part of transcendental philosophy. It shows not
only that there are pure conceptions à priori, but
it distinguishes also how many there are of them,—
how they spring up, whether the understanding
cognizes through them alone, how far they may be
applied, and if and how, consequently, they limit
the understanding. This science stands in the
same light, in regard to pure conceptions à priori,
that Transcendental Æsthetick does to pure intuitions à priori. It has only to do with the laws of the
understanding and of reason, so far simply as it
has reference to objects à priori ; and it differs in
this way from Logic Universal which refers indif-
ferently to cognitions empirical as well as to those
appertaining to pure reason.

Universal Logic again is divided into what is Analytick and what is Dialectick. Analytick, by dis-
secting, discovers all the operation of reason which
we perform in thinking in general. It is therefore
an Analytick of the understanding and of reason,
and is justly named the Logic of Truth, because it
contains the necessary rules of all (formal) truth,
and without which our cognition is, with regard to
the objects, untrue in itself. Should this merely
theoretical and universal doctrine be used as a
practical art, that is, as an Organon, it would become
a Dialectick or Logic of Appearance, which arises
from a mere abuse of the Analytick, when, according to the bare logical form, the appearance of a
true cognition, whose marks must however be

taken from the agreement with the objects, and consequently from the matter, is fabricated.

In Transcendental Logic we isolate the understanding, as in Transcendental Æsthetick we isolate sensibility, and we extract merely that part of thought from our cognition, which has its origin solely in the understanding ; and the use of this pure cognition rests upon this as its condition, that objects can be given to us in intuition to which the pure cognition can be applied. Care must be taken in making use of these pure understanding-cognitions and principles, that a material use is not made of what is merely formal. When transcendental Analytick is considered as an Organon of universal and unlimited use, instead of a Canon of judgment in an empirical sense, it falls into mistakes and error and the use becomes dialectical. The second part of Transcendental Logic will be a criticism of this dialectical Appearance to expose its fallacy and correct its errors.

Transcendental Analytick, then, is the dissection of our whole cognition, à priori, into the elements of the pure cognition of the understanding, and the following are the conditions :—That the conceptions must be pure and not empirical conditions—that they do not belong to intuition or sensibility, but to thought and understanding, and that they are elemental, and not derived or composed,—that they fill up the whole field of the pure understanding, which is a unity, self-subsisting and self-sufficient. This part of Transcendental Logic consists of two divisions, one of which concerns the conceptions, the other the principles of the pure understanding. Transcendental Analytick is termed the dissection of the understanding itself, in order to investigate the possibility of conceptions a priori, and to look at them as they lie prepared, as it were, in the human intellect, until developed by experience, whence we again liberate them from such empirical conditions as attach to them when seen in action. The different kind of judgments afford us the means of ascertaining which are the functions of the understanding.

If we can expose with certainty the functions of unity in judgments, which judgments are the mediate cognitions of objects, we can then find the functions of the understanding, which we before explained as a non-sensible cognition faculty. Now all functions of thought in judgments are found reducible to four heads, each of which is again divided into three classes. These are—

I.

Quantity of Judgments.

Universal.
Particular.
Individual.

II.	III.	IV.
Quality.	*Relation.*	*Modality.*
Affirmative.	Categorical.	Problematical.
Negative.	Hypothetical.	Assertorical.
Infinite.	Disjunctive.	Apodictical.

Thus it is in making abstraction of the object as to which a judgment is given, that we arrive at form; and when we are acquainted with all the forms and modes of judgment, we are then acquainted with all the forms of the understanding.

Now just as many pure understanding-conceptions arise which refer, à priori, to objects of intuition in general, as there are logical functions of all the possible judgments just detailed, and these four understanding-conceptions are what are termed the Categories, and they are the following :—

TABLE OF CATEGORIES.

I. *Of Quantity.*	II. *Of Quality.*
Unity.	Reality.
Plurality.	Negation.
Totality.	Limitation.

III.
Of Relation.

Inherence and Subsistence (Substantia et Accidens.)
Causality and Dependence (Cause and Effect).
Community (Reciprocity between the Agent and the Patient).

IV.
Of Modality.

Possibility.	Impossibility.
Existence.	Non-existence.
Necessity.	Contingence.

Such is the enumeration of all the originally pure conceptions of that synthesis which the understanding contains within itself à priori, and by reason of which it simply is pure understanding, inasmuch as by means of the said pure conceptions only can it comprehend anything in the diversity of the intuition. Aristotle had an idea of this faculty of the understanding, but it was an incorrect one, as he added some conceptions and omitted others which disfigured the catalogue. To this table of the categories, Kant added another list, which he called Predicables, but which he merely indicated without developing.

The existence of the Categories and their number being deduced and proved, the next question naturally is as to their application, for without this they are nothing more than inert capacities remaining in total inaction. To us they are absolutely non-existing, so long as they have not been called into operation by external objects. Now, in order to know an object, two things are necessary, the intuition by which the object is given, and the idea by which this same object, corresponding to the intuition, is converted into thought. This is the operation of the understanding. Kant, in imitation of certain jurists, calls the right by which we establish the connexion, the Deduction, which in a *general sense* means the proof of claim, or a claim of right. In a *particular sense* it signifies the legitimatizing, if it may be so expressed, of a representation, or proof of the right to use the same, or that the representation possesses sense, meaning, and objective validity; and more especially that it is not void, but refers to objects in reality. Then again there is another distinction between empirical and transcendental Deduction. It is the former which explains the validity of an empirical representation through the proof of its origin from experience itself, showing that the representation necessarily refers to the object, since the one makes the other possible. Transcendental Deduction, on the other hand, shows that a representation can be referred, à priori to an object, and without having its origin from experience, can still be valid as to the objects themselves : and our Author contends that it was because Locke did not see the necessity of something in the understanding previous to experience, namely, conditions à priori, that he was led into error. Meeting with pure conceptions of the understanding in experience, this great philosopher derives the same from experience, and he ventured in this way upon attempts at cognitions, which extend far beyond the limits of experience. Hume saw that in order to do this, it was necessary (which Kant also contends is the case) that these conceptions should have their origin à priori. But not being able to explain how it was possible that the understanding should be compelled to think conceptions, which are not in themselves conjoined in the understanding, yet as necessarily conjoined in the object, he deduced the same from experience, or subjective necessity, or Habit. It did not enter into his imagination, that possibly the understanding itself, by means of these conceptions, was the author of the experience. But he acted more consistently than Locke in this respect in declaring that with the conceptions in question and the principles they gave rise to, it was impossible to go out beyond the limits of experience. The fact, however, of both Pure Mathematics and general Physics proving cognitions à priori to exist, overthrows the system of both of these great philosophers.

Synthesis or conjunction is the operation of the understanding alone, and we can represent to ourselves nothing as conjoined in the object, unless we ourselves have previously conjoined it. This is an act of self-activity. Analysis is posterior to

Synthesis, for only as conjoined by the understanding can anything be presented to us, and
admit of being decomposed. Conjunction is the
synthetic unity of the Multiplex or Diverse. The
representation of this unity does not arise out of
the composition ; it precedes every thing, and therefore is to be distinguished especially from the Category of Unity.

As in Transcendental Æsthetick, or the first division of the work, it is declared that all diversity of
what appertains to sensibility, or what appertains
to the domain of sense in general must stand as to
intuitions, under the formal conditions of space and
time ; so the highest principle with reference to
the understanding must stand under an original
Unity of Apperception. And this is the " I think"
which must be able to accompany all my representations. It is pure or original Apperception. It
accompanies every other. Self-consciousness is at
the bottom of all my representations, for otherwise
they would not be mine. Analytical unity of
apperception is opposed to the synthetical unity.
The distinction as laid down is a little difficult
to be understood when expressed simply in the
language of Kant, but when divested of technicality,
the difference is obvious. Analytical unity is
that by means of which conceptions are thought
as conjoined. If the Understanding thinks two
conceptions as conjoined in one judgment, the representation by which they are thought as conjoined is analytical unity. The conception of a
black Dish, for instance, is an analytical unity, inasmuch as the representation of the conjunction of
the two conceptions, black and dish, in one judgment, is that the " Dish is black." The idea of
man in general is an analytical unity, as the term

applies to men of every colour. It is called the
Analytical unity of apperception or consciousness,
by reason of many conceptions being conjoined
through it in one consciousness. For instance, if I
think of the colour red, I represent to myself a
quality which is common to different representations; all of which are thought as red. It is the
analytical unity of consciousness which makes a
representation into a common conception. It is
opposed to the synthetical unity of consciousness,
by which I represent to myself the part-represen-
tations as conjoined, *in one object*, which always
presupposes intuition, and not in a judgment, which
is an analytical proceeding. It is also a similar
act when I attach the colour, as for instance, Red-
ness in general to several objects, but it is a synthetical one, to think the colour itself, when diversity
of intuitions is thought or envisaged as conjoined.
The pure conception of the understanding, or the
Category, is synthetic unity, because through it
different representations in an intuition are conjoined in one conception, whether of Quantity
Quality, Reality, or Substance. The principle of
the synthetical unity of the apperception is the
highest principle of all use of the understanding,
and leads to the logical form of all judgments, which
consist in the objective unity of the conceptions
therein contained ; and we perceive that the diversity contained in the intuition, which I call mine, is
represented by the synthesis of the understanding
as belonging to the necessary unity of self-consciousness. This occurs through the category which
shows that the empirical consciousness of a given
diversity of an intuition is subject, just in the same
way, to a pure self-intuition à priori, as empirical
intuition is to a pure sensible one, which also takes

place à priori. But at the same time that the category is spoken of as being that by which alone unity is given to the diversity of a given intuition generally, it must not be overlooked, that the category is of no other use for the cognition of things, than so far as it has application to objects of experience. Two parts belong to cognitions, first the conception in which the object is thought, or the category; and secondly the intuition whereby it is given ; for if a corresponding intuition to conception could not be given, it might, as to its form, be thought, but being without an object, no cognition of it would be at all possible. The thought or the thinking of an object in general by means of the category or pure understanding-conception can only become cognition in us, so far as the same has reference to objects of the senses.

It must at the same time be observed that Synthesis is divided into two kinds, Speciosa and Intellectualis. By the former, or speciosa or figurative, is meant that which is possible and necessary à priori, in contradistinction to that which, in respect of the diversity of an intuition in general, would be thought in the mere category, and is termed on its part synthesis intellectualis, or conjunction of the understanding. Both are transcendental, not merely because they themselves are à priori, but because they form the basis of the possibility of other cognition à priori. The figurative synthesis is the Synthesis of the Imagination,*

---

* In the first edition of the Critick, when speaking of the Faculty of the Imagination, Kant shews that in order to present a whole, it was necessary to see each of the several parts, and to collect them successively and finally to unite them in one image. This was in fact Imagination. The Conjunction or union of these was the

which is the faculty of representing an object without its presence in the intuition.

It is at this point that, after having exposed the different kinds of syntheses, Kant digresses into an explanation of a position which he had laid down in an earlier part of his work, in some degree, dogmatically, in order at this stage of his system to justify the assertion that the I may be both active and passive.

But to understand this it will be necessary to consider rather more in detail the characteristics or qualities of the I, which being the foundation of all other acquisitions, requires to be investigated in its innermost nature and capacity. It is the I, then, which connects in man all his intuitions and thoughts. There is nothing beyond this I that is either diverse or multiplex, but it is that wherewith all that is diverse in the intuition and the conception as therein conjoined, is represented. This I, however, does not envisage its own self, for it is neither an intuition-faculty, which would be, as it were, something super-sensible or intellectual; nor is it an object given to the intuition, but it is merely the ground of the conjunction of the diverse in an

---

" Synthesis of the Apprehension of the Intuition ;" and as this act of apprehension was successive, and it was necessary to reproduce one part before passing to another, the Imagination became necessarily a reproduction-faculty, and the Synthesis of the Reproduction in the intuition thereby occurs. This reproduction would be of no avail unless we were conscious that each part was the same before and after the reproduction, and from this resulted the synthesis of the cognition of the idea, so that objective cognition in experience is only possible by means of a triple synthesis, that of the Apperception in the Intuition, that of the Reproduction in the Imagination, and that of Cognition in the idea by means of consciousness. The analysis, in this form at least, is omitted or changed in all the editions of the Critick that succeeded to the first.

object. I call all representations mine, because I
am one and the same person who conjoins them.
In this manner the I is termed the *original synthetic* unity of the apperception, or consciousness :
original, because this representation of the I can be
derived from nothing else, *synthetic*, since it lies at
the foundation or root of all conjunction or synthesis, and makes this same synthesis possible.
The representation I, or I think, is the manifesta-
tion of a spontaneity (not the being-affected state
of the sensibility), and it is termed the transcendental unity of self-consciousness, in order thereby
to show that without the same, no conjunction is
possible à priori, and that it precedes all experience,
and yet is not derived from experience.

As Space and Time are forms of all intuitions,
so, according to the sense Kant attaches to the I,
does this I appear to be the form of the pure original
conceptions of the understanding, and to lie at the
bottom of them, so that the difference of the two I's
is rendered comprehensible by referring the one to
reason and the other to sense.

The I that thinks is rational, the I that is thought
is empirical.   Thus unity is the original character-
istic of the understanding or mind, or by whatever
name the intellectual principle in man is denominated, and every thing is presented to it as a unity ;
consequently, conjunction or synthesis or unity,
is the first condition of thought ; but then again it
must not be forgotten, that this Unity, I think, lying
at the foundation of the human mind as elemental
principle, is not to be confounded with that category
of Unity, which exists in the table of the categories,
and is the first division of the category of Quantity.   The Unity now in question is a higher Unity

than the categorical one, and is to be found at the
root of the possibility of the understanding itself
in its logical use. It is independent of all conditions of sensible intuition, and is the principle
of the original synthetic Unity of apperception ;
whilst categories, it may be repeated, are of no
value to procure Knowledge, excepting so far as
they apply to objects presented to us by experience. They are all forms of Thought.

To think an object, and to know an object are
two distinct things. We have the conception
whereby a thing is thought, and that is the
category ; and we have the intuition whereby the
thing is given,—for could an intuition corresponding to the conception not be given, the latter
would be a thought, as to its form, but without any
object, and by means of it no cognition at all of an
object would be possible, since, so far as I know,
there was neither any thing, nor could be any
thing, to which *my* thought could be applied.
Sensible intuition is either *pure*, that is, it is space
or time, or it is *empirical*, that is, that which is
immediately represented in space and time as real
by means of sensation. Through the determination
of the first we obtain cognition à priori of objects,
as in Mathematics, but yet only according to
their form as phenomena, and thus every thing is reduced ultimately to experience, so far as knowledge
is concerned, the categories themselves affording
us no cognition of objects, except through their
possible application to empirical intuition, which is
only another name for experience. To think is to
unite several ideas in the unity of conscience, and
thought and judgment are valid when they are
confirmable to the axiom of Identity, whether they

have or have not an object corresponding to them in the reality. Thought can teach us nothing, but to know an object is to have an intuition corresponding to the idea ; and a pure idea cannot be known except inasmuch as it refers to an intuition which is sensible.

The difference of the internal sense and of consciousness, according to our author, has been overlooked by Psychologists, and has led to confusion and embarrassment. The internal sense is time, and this internal sense is determined by the understanding, or, it may be said, by ourselves, and this determination takes place according to the synthesis which the understanding thinks for the internal intuition. Pure apperception, or consciousness is the source and principle of all synthesis, and whether an object is given to it or not, it refers à priori to the variety of intuitions in general. The internal sense, on the other hand, is the simple form of the intuitions, and it contains no synthesis, and consequently no determinate intuition, for this is only possible by a transcendental synthesis, or by the influence of the understanding upon the internal sense. It is thus that we cannot represent to ourselves a line, nor a circle, nor a triangle, without tracing it visibly, and the three dimensions of space, Length, Breadth, and Thickness, are designated by drawing one line which is perpendicular to another.

In general Logic all *content* of cognition being abstracted, its business is to expose analytically the *form* of cognition in conceptions, judgments, and conclusions, and thereby to establish formal rules of the use of the understanding, but with all this it cannot give any precepts for the faculty of judgment. Transcendental Logic is differently circumstanced ;

and it would seem as if it had for its peculiar province to correct and secure, by means of determinate rules, the faculty of judgment, in the use of the pure understanding.   Transcendental philosophy goes even further than this, for besides the rule, (or rather the general condition for rules) which is given in the pure use of the understanding, it can at once indicate à priori the case wherein the rule is to be applied.   It has a preference over all other branches of science, excepting mathematics, inasmuch as it treats of conceptions which are to refer to their objects à priori ; and the objective validity of these which are the categories, cannot be demonstrated à posteriori.   But at the same time that transcendental science does this, it must likewise expose as general or sufficient characteristics, the conditions under which such objects can be given, in accordance with such conceptions.   If it were not so, these conceptions or categories would be without content, and mere logical forms, and not pure conceptions of the understanding.

The first point then to be considered (and this is the work of Transcendental Analytick) is, how this pure conception of the understanding can be used, or what is the sensible condition, under which alone it can be of avail.   The next enquiry then to be made is into those synthetic judgments which flow from the pure conceptions of the understanding under conditions à priori, and which lie at the foundation of all other cognitions à priori.   The one may be called the Schematism, the other the principles of the pure Understanding.   This forms another of the great divisions of the work before us.

In all subsumptions of an object under a conception, the representation of the one must be homogeneous with the other, or the conception itself must contain that which is represented in the object to be subsumed under it. The empirical conception of a *plate* is homogeneous, with the pure geometrical one of a *circle*—the roundness which is envisaged in the plate is thought in the conception of a circle. But pure conceptions of the understanding are quite heterogeneous with those that are empirical, and they can never be met with in any intuition ; and to render the application of the categories to phenomena possible, we must adopt a medium which shall be itself pure, and yet be on the one hand, (in reference to the understanding) intellectual, and on the other, sensible. The transcendental doctrine of Judgment is to shew how this is to be effected, and the representation itself is termed a Transcendental Schema.

The conception of the understanding or the category contains pure synthetical union of the diverse generally, and Time, as the formal condition of the diversity of the internal sense, consequently, of the conjunction of all representations, contains a diverse à priori in the pure intuition. Now a transcendental determination of time, which constitutes the unity of the category, is so far homogeneous with it, as it is *general*, and rests upon a rule à priori, and this transcendental determination, on the other hand, is so far homogeneous with the phenomenon, as time is contained in every empirical representation of the diverse, and in this way an application of the category to phenomena is possible by means of this transcendental determination of time, which as the schema of the conceptions of the understanding, operates as a medium of the subsumption of the phenomena under the category.

The term Schema, however, is not to be confounded with the Greek word, *Image*, from which it is derived, which is something particular or specific or individual, and therefore empirical, whereas the word schema in the present philosophical sense is generic, and includes in its meaning what is universal in its character; as for instance, the conception of man, which is subsumed under that of mortal, and the conception of ball under that of a sphere. A polyhedron drawn is an image of the figure which I have in view when I entertain its idea. A polyhedron in general is not an image but only a rule, in order to represent this figure by an image, which never can attain to the idea that exists within us. The medium which renders categories homogeneous with intuitions, is Time. This is the connection between the pure conceptions of the understanding and objects; categories rendered sensible by time are schemata, and these are products of the imagination. All our ideas possess a schema as their foundation, but they have not images of the object, for no image of an object can entirely coincide with the pure idea. To the figure before mentioned, the polyhedron, for example, this in its generality can never have an adequate or complete image, because the image cannot attain to the generality of my idea, and would be limited to a part only of the idea. The image could only represent a tetrahedron, an hexedron, or an oxhedron, whilst the idea of a polyhedron in general comprehends in itself all these figures. The schema of a polyhedron can only exist in the idea, and it indicates a rule of the synthesis of the imagination with relation to figures in space.

As there are as many classes of schemata as there are categories, we shall under the schema of Quantity necessarily find Unity, Plurality, and Universality. This schema is Number in general, or the synthesis of time, as One, Several, and the Whole.

The schema of quality is a degree in general, or the synthesis of sensations in time. Reality is that to which sensation corresponds in every intuition, and as there is an infinite number of degrees between sensation and the absence of sensation, we have in the one case Limitation, and in the other Negation, or the state of the transition of the degree of intensity of a sensation until its final distinction. The schema of Relation is the relationship of sensations between themselves in the order of time. Substance is the perdurability of a reality in time, or that which remains whilst all its accidents change. Causality is the determinate succession of realities in time, so that when one event occurs, another necessarily follows. Community or concurrence is the co-existence of realities in space, so that one determines the place of the other. The schema of Modality is the mode of existence of sensations in time, or the complex of time. Possibility is the idea of an object being able to exist only in time. Existence is the being of a reality in a given time. Necessity the idea of an object, always existing in time. Hence it will be seen how the connexion of a variety, and therefore the representation of an object, is possible. The categories, as pure intellectual conceptions, could not effect this; but the schemata being employed as media the necessary unity of the given variety is represented. The categories rendered sensible by time are the schemata, and all objects are given by their means. We may think a thing through the categories, but we cannot say any thing of it, or attribute any predicate to it, and the pure origin of the category does not assist in saying what an object is, because we must have an intuition before we can make anything of it. We cannot know anything of Noumena, or Things in themselves, but only of Phenomena, or Things as they appear. Time being the form of the internal sense, schemata produce the synthesis of the intuition of the internal sense, and they are the only mode by which reality can be given to the categories in establishing their relationship to objects. But although the schemata of sensibility give reality to the categories, yet they at the same time limit them, and the schema being the sensible conception of an object in unison with the category, it is evident that schemata only represent things as they appear, and not as they are, which the categories, in their pure signification, would do, were it possible that there could be an application of them in this sense. Without schemata, the categories are simply functions of the understanding for conceptions, but they represent no object. Meaning comes to them from sensibility, and this, whilst it realizes, at the same time necessarily restricts the understanding.

Having thus disposed of the Schemata, it will be necessary to investigate the second portion of the division of the faculties of the understanding, and to explain what is meant by Principles of the pure understanding, and with this one main branch of the subject will be completed. Analytical Judgments have been shown to be those which are tested by the principle of non-contradiction. The principle of their legitimacy consists in this, that the idea of the predicate is contained in the subject, as for instance, " Bodies are extended," where the predicate extended is contained in the idea, "body." The two ideas also are identical, the predicate, in fact, doing nothing but developing and extending the subject. But with synthetical judgments the case is quite different. In these the subject does not contain the predicate, and this may or may not agree with the subject without there being any contradiction, and without the affirmation or negation being contrary to the Axiom of contradiction spoken of; hence it is evident that this is not the principle of synthetic, as it was of analytical judgments.

In the analytical judgment, I stop at the given conception, in order to make out something with respect to it. If it is to be affirmative, I merely attribute to this conception that which was already thought in it. If it is to be negative, I exclude only the contrary thereof from it. But in synthetical judgments I must go beyond the given conception, in order to consider, in reference to the same, something quite different from that which was thought in it,—which, therefore, is never either a relationship of identity or of contradiction,—and whereby in the judgment in itself, neither the truth nor the error can be seen.

Experience arises when together with the necessary unity of consciousness, variety of the empirical intuition is thought, and such experience reposes upon the synthetical unity of phenomena, without which it would never be cognition, but merely a rhapsody or unconnected body of perceptions which would not arrange themselves together in any context according to the rules of an absolutely connected consciousness.

Experience, therefore, has lying even at its foundation, the principles of its form à priori, or general rules of unity in the synthesis of phenomena, and the highest principle of all synthetical judgments is that every object is subject to the necessary conditions of the synthetical unity of the diversity of the intuitions in a possible experience. The conditions of possibility of experience in general are at the same time conditions of the possibility of the objects of experience, and they have for this reason objective validity in a synthetical judgment à priori.

That there are synthetical principles of the pure understanding, is clear from the fact that experience being general or valid for every body, and this experience, consisting in the representation of a necessary connexion of the variety of empirical intuitions, having only been rendered possible by the application of the categories to intuition, the understanding must therefore contain within itself these rules which are necessary to determine the cases of application.

The principles of the pure understanding are divided like the categories and schemata, into four classes, and they comprehend, first, as relating to the principle of Quantity, the Axioms of Intuition. Secondly, in reference to that of Quality, the Anticipations of Perception. Thirdly, with respect to Relation, the Analogies of Experience. Fourthly, in regard to Modality, the Postulates of Empirical Thought in general. These principles are not all of the same nature, the two former being those which are termed *constitutive* or absolutely necessary, inasmuch as they concern intuitions without which the object would not be given, deter-

D

mining really what the phenomenon contains with
reference to the form of the intuition. The two
latter on the other hand are merely *discursive* or produced by the ideas, and are only necessary under
the condition of a possible experience which is
always contingent. These are also termed Dynamical, in opposition to the former, which are designated Mathematical, but without its being intended
to limit the meaning to the principles of the mathematics on the one hand, or to those of physical dy-
namics on the other; but only to those of the pure
understanding in relation to the internal sense,
without any distinction of the representations therein
given. The title is allotted rather in consideration
of their application than their content.*

It is to be here borne in mind, that the point
under consideration is the possibility of experience
itself, and the mode in which it is practicable.
But it must not be supposed that the synthetical
principles à priori in question have meaning irres-
pective of sensible application. They afford no rules
as to what objects are absolutely, without reference
to given intuition, and to the form of the internal
sense, as condition of the synthetical unity of the
intuition. The laws of the understanding are in
ourselves, that is to say, in our understanding, and
they are not derived from elsewhere: and the pos-

---

* A subtle distinction is made by Kant in the connexion of the
variety of empirical intuition according to the categories. This is
stated to be of two kinds, one a connexion of the Homogeneous, or
Compositio, the other of the Heterogeneous or *Nexus;* all *con-
junctio* belonging to either of these classes. The one is mathematical, the other dynamical, and this last is subdivided into the physical
and metaphysical. *Compositio* is a square divided into two triangles
by a diagonal. *Nexus* is when one thing necessarily belongs to
another, as accident to substance, or effect to cause.

sibility of experience itself reposes upon the synthetic unity of phenomena or Ideas à priori or
categories.

In the division of the principles of the pure understanding, it has just been observed, that " the
Axioms of Intuition" are at the head of the list,
and the principle of these is that " all intuitions
are extensive Quantities," that is, that they possess extensive quantities, or as it may be otherwise
expressed, it is impossible to represent to ourselves
any thing if it be not in space and time.

The proof adduced is this, that all phenomena
contain, according to form, an intuition in space
and time, lying at the foundation of the whole of
them à priori. They can therefore only be apprehended or received into empirical consciousness
through the synthesis of the Diverse, whereby the
representations of a determined space or time are
generated. This synthesis is the conjunction of a
Diverse-homogeneous, and its representation is
the conception of Quantity. All phenomena are,
in fact, quantities, and they are extensive quantities,
the character of this kind of quantity being that
the representation of the parts renders possible the
representation of the whole, and so far, consequently,
the one precedes the other. I can represent to
myself no line, however small it may be, without
drawing it at least in idea—thereby deducing from
one point all the parts in succession, and so dis-
secting as it were the intuition. And in respect of
time, the same process takes place, for with regard
to the smallest portion of it, I therein think to
myself only the successive progression from one
moment to another, and in this way by means of all
the portions of time, and their addition, a deter-

minate quantity of time is ultimately produced.
The simple intuition in all phenomena must be
either space or time, and each phenomenon is, as
intuition, an extensive quantity, because only,
through successive quantities from part to part
can it be recognized in apprehension.

The second principle of the understanding, the
principle of Quality, is termed " Anticipations of
Perception;" and here it is shown that " in all phenomena, the Real which is an object of sensation
or a sensible object, possesses intensive quantity,
that is, it has a degree:" or in other words it may be
said, that all our sensations have a certain degree of
intensity. The proof of this rests upon the fact, that
each sensation filling up only one moment, the
reality of phenomenon is only perceived at once,
and not successively. But between each sensation
or reality in the phenomenon and negation, there is
a continual connection of many possible intermediate sensations, the difference of which from one to
the other is always smaller than the difference between the given one and zero, or total negation. Every
sensation, however small it may be, has in fact a
degree or intensive quantity, which may always be
further diminished ; and between reality and negation there is a continual connexion of possible
realities, and of possible smaller perceptions. Every
colour, for instance, as red or blue, has a degree,
which, however delicate it may be, is never the
most delicate ; and it is the same with the qualities
of Heat, Weight, &c. generally. This property of
quantities is termed their continuity, and space
and time are *Quanta continua*, because no parts
thereof can be given without the same being in-
cluded within points or instants as limits. Space

therefore consists of spaces, and Time of times.
Phenomena are all continuous quantities, extensive
with reference to their intuition, and intensive
as regards their mere perception. Between the
reality in the phenomenon and the negation there
may be any number of degrees, the total vanishing
of the reality at any determinate point, not being
provable either as to space or time. With respect to what constitutes the empirical in a phenomenon, this cannot be known except à posteriori;
but that a phenomenon must have a reality, we
know à priori, and from looking at the nature of experience we anticipate what is to arise, and by this
principle of anticipation, the determination of the
particular realities belonging to objects of experience becomes possible.

The third principle of the understanding or Relation is designated the " Analogies of experience,"
and here it has to be shown that experience is only
possible by means of the representation of a necessary connexion of perceptions, and these analogies
are divided into three classes, termed the Principle
of the Perdurability of substance ; Succession of
time according to the laws of causality ; Coexistence
according to the laws of reciprocity or Community.

With regard to the proof of one principle of
this division, or that experience is only possible by
means of a necessary connexion of apprehensions,
it must be evident that experience is only empirical
cognition, or a synthesis of perceptions, which itself
is not contained in the perception, and the cognition
of phenomena is only possible by means of synthetic unity ; so that, in order to determine the
existence of objects in any given time, it is necessary that the synthesis thereof must be possible

in time. Now as the synthesis of apprehension
can only occur in time, the variety in experience
must occur in general according to the three modes
of time, and which are those of Perdurability, Succession, and Co-existence, and these three laws,
which are those of all the relationships of time in
phenomena, will precede and render possible all
experience, whereby to each phenomenon, its existence, in respect of the unity of time, can be determined.

The first Analogy asserting the principle of the
perdurability of substance, necessarily maintains
that, in all change of phenomena the substance is
permanent, and that its quantum in nature is
neither diminished nor increased.

The proof is analyzed with great dexterity,
showing that there can be no such thing as empty
time, time being only capable of representation
when it is filled. For co-existence is simultaneousness, and succession and determinations of time can
only be represented by means of a substratum, which
represents time in general, and in which all change
or co-existence can be perceived by means of the
relationship of phenomena to this substratum in the
apprehension. Now substance is the substratum
of all that is real, or of all that belongs to the
existence of things, in the which substance all that
appertains to existence can be thought only as determination. There must be an invariable and
durable principle in time, whereof succession and
simultaneousness are only modifications, and consequently all phenomena must have this principle,
which is the object itself. No relationships can be
given by time itself, which is in itself nothing, and
cannot be perceived ; and they cannot be given by

our perceptions, for the synthesis of these is always
successive.   It cannot therefore teach us whether
the diverse in phenomena, as object of experience
is co-existent or successive, provided something
does not lie at the foundation which is or exists
always, that is to say, which is something fixed and
permanent, and as to which all change and co-existence are nothing else but so many modi of time
wherein the permanent exists, because only in the
permanent are the relationships of time possible.
The determinations of a substance which are nothing
else but its particular modes of existing, are termed
Accidents, and these are always real because they
concern the existence of the substance.   Upon
permanence alone can we ground the conception of
change.   Change is one mode of existence, which
follows upon another of the same object, and therefore all that changes is permanent, its state alone
varies.   Neither absolute rise or origin nor extinction can be a possible perception ; for if it be
assumed that something begins to be, there must
be a point of time wherein it was not, but only a
void time.   No object of perception now is an ex-
tinct time, for this would be to suppose an empirical representation of time when there was no phenomenon.   Permanence is thus a necessary condition under which alone phenomena, as things or
objects, are determinable in a possible experience.
What the empirical criterium of this necessary
permanence may be, and of the substantiality of
the phenomena, will be remarked hereafter.
    The second Analogy is the Principle of produc-
tion or of succession, according to the laws of
causality, and this corresponds to the second of the
three modes of Time, and the import of it is, that

"all changes occur according to the law of connexion of cause and effect." This answers to the principle of *Nihil est sine ratione sufficiente*, as the preceding law did to the dictum *Gigni de nihilo nihil, in nihilum nil posse reverti.* As the first Analogy showed that all the phenomena of the succession of time are only changes, the present indicates that all changes occur according to the law of the synthesis of cause and effect, or in other words, every phenomena which appears supposes another to which it succeeds, by virtue of a necessary law. Now what is necessary must arise from a category, and we see in the table of the categories, that under the head of Relation, the second in that division is the one of causality and dependence. Succession of ideas may differ in different individuals, but if change is involved, that is, if change be part of the apprehension, then the idea is objectively valid for every one; for instance, in looking at a house or a statue, the apprehension of it may begin with one man at the roof or the head, or with another at the foundation or foot, but if the conception carries with it a necessity of synthetic unity, this being a pure conception of the understanding, or a category, the same does not lie in the perception. Such a conception is that of the relationship of Cause and Effect. I perceive that phenomena succeed one another, or I connect two opposite states of substance in time. All this takes place in my own mind, and the connexion is either voluntary, that is, it remains with me which state shall be first, and which last; or it is necessary, that is, I am conscious that the one state must ever be the first, and the other the last. In the first case, the connexion is subjective, or it is

in my imagination, and not in the objects; but in
the second case, the subjective connexion is changed
into an objective one, or it is represented not
merely as to be found in my mind, but is at the
same time in the phenomena, or the objects of experience. If, consequently, the objective succession of things is to be distinguished from the subjective, and the first not held to be the last, this must
arise from the principle of Necessity, and this
again brings us back to the same point, that necessity is only possible à priori ; and the connexion
discovered must be a work of the understanding.
When objects are represented in space, the order
of succession is then voluntary, and when they are
represented as successive in time, the order is necessary. As to the question respecting the cause
of changes, great error may arise and false motions
be attributed, but it is the conception of cause in
general, or that there is a cause for every change,
which enters into our consideration here; and as
this is a necessary law of thought, this is, as it was
before stated to be, itself a Category. We are certainly ignorant à priori of the definite cause of any
particular change, but we are thoroughly convinced
that every change has a cause. Neither can this
conception of cause be obtained empirically, because then time and space would be of empirical
origin, which is what transcendental philosophy
positively denies. If then we can have only an
idea of one thing after another, and if such is a
necessary consequence, it is evident that it occurs
according to a positive law, and this law is that of
cause and effect. This law of causality cannot
be borrowed from experience, because, as just
mentioned, it is a necessary law ; for unless it were

so, it would be impossible to conceive the necessary
succession of perceptions, and to distinguish that
necessary succession which is objective, from the
subjective succession of perceptions.   Hence the
principle, *In mundo non datur fatum.*

When two apprehensions follow one another, it
is evident that this is nothing but the succession of
two representations, and this is subjective, and yet
to this subjective act we attribute continually
reference to an object, and this arises, it may be
again repeated, from the category, for without it,
the objective relationship would be merely a subjective play of the imagination, and we should
merely say that one apprehension followed upon
another, but not that it was necessarily so.   In
thinking of cause and effect, or the law of causality, continual reference is made to what is termed,
Power, Action, Force, and Substance ; and it is
thereby meant that where there is action, consequently activity and force, there also is substance,
and in this substance alone must the seat of that
fruitful source of phenomena, action, be found.
Action signifies the relationship of the subject
of causality to the effect ; and since the effect
consists in that which happens, consequently in
the *Mutable* which time indicates according to
succession, the last subject of this is the *Permanent* as the substratum of the changeable, that
is, the substance.   For according to the principles of causality, actions are always the first
foundation of all change of phenomena, and cannot
therefore lie in a subject which itself changes,
because otherwise other actions and another subject
determining such change would be required.   In
consequence of this, action shows as a sufficient

empirical criterium, substantiality, without its being necessary first of all to seek the permanence of this substance by means of compared perceptions. The first subject of the causality of all origin and extinction cannot itself, in the field of phenomena, arise or perish. This runs into empirical necessity and permanency of existence, and consequently into the conception of substance as phenomenon. When an origin arises from an extraneous cause, it is termed creation, which cannot be admitted amongst phenomena as an event, for its possibility would annihilate the unity of experience; although, when things are considered not as phenomena, but as things in themselves and objects of the mere understanding, then, notwithstanding they are substances, they may be regarded as dependent upon an extraneous cause, in respect of their existence. But this would not be phenomena, as possible objects of experience. In conclusion, it should not be overlooked, that concomitance, as well as succession, belongs to cause and effect; for though one position of causal-connexion amongst phenomena is limited in our formula to the succession of their series, we still find, in the use of the same position, that it suits with their concomitancy, and can at the same time be cause and effect. There is, for instance, warmth in a room which cannot be met with in the open air. I look for the cause, and find it in a heated stove. Now this stove, as cause, with warmth` as its effect, are coexistent, and consequently there is here no succession of series, according to time, between cause and effect, but they are contemporaneous; and yet the law in question holds good. The greater part of the effective causes in nature are together in time with their effects ; and the succession of time in the latter only arises through this, that the cause cannot produce the whole effect in a moment. But in the moment when this first begins, it is always co-existent with the causality of its cause, because if that (the cause) had ceased to be a moment previously, this (the effect) would not at all have taken place. We must also here particularly observe, that we are here to look at the order of time, and not the flow of time—the relationship remaining, although no time have elapsed. The time between the causality of the cause and its immediate effect, may be vanishing away, (therefore be co-existently the effect,) but still the relationship of one to the other always remains determinable according to time. If I consider a ball which lies upon a stuffed cushion, and makes an impression thereon, as a cause, it is contemporaneous with the effect. But I still distinguish both, through the relationships of time of the dynamic connexion of the two. For if I place the ball upon the cushion, the dent succeeds to its previous smooth shape, but if the cushion have (I know not whence) a dent, a leaden ball does not succeed to that.

Succession is, therefore, absolutely the single empirical criterium of effect, in reference to the causality of the cause which precedes. The glass is the cause of the rise of water above its horizontal surface, although both phenomena are co-existent. For as soon as I have drawn this water with the glass out of a larger vessel, something ensues, that is to say, change of the horizontal state which it had there (in the vessel), into a concave one, which it assumes in the glass.

Hence we see that it is the Intellect which connects. One species of this connection is, that it makes some of the realities of time to follow upon some other realities agreeably to the laws of its constitution. This species of connexion considered separately comprehends the categories of cause and effect, but applied to time it is the schema of this category, and it presents such connexion as inhering to the realities of time.

The law of continuity, or the proposition that in the transition from one state to the other, no change can be the smallest, comes under this analogy. It is found à priori, because all changes occur in time, and each perception only renders perceptible the succession of time. To find the law, we anticipate our perceptions in time, in order to conceive how the succession of time occurs in general. All the determinations of time therefore being à priori, the law itself must be so necessarily.

The third Analogy is the principle of coexistence according to the laws of reciprocity or community, and the law is that " all substances, so far as they can be perceived in space in the same time, are in thorough reciprocalness of action, and so far as they are coexistent, that they stand in absolute community or reciprocalness with one another, or that they are in thorough action or reaction." It has been observed in speaking of and explaining the second principle or analogy, that in the succession of phenomena the perception of one thing cannot follow upon the perception of another reciprocally, but is determined in the mind. In the analogy, however, now to be explained, the contrary occurs, as for instance, in looking at the earth or moon, it is immaterial which is the first percep-

tion in order. It is of no consequence whether
I begin my perception first with the moon, and
afterwards the earth, or conversely, first with the
earth, and then with the moon ; and because
the perceptions of these objects follow one another
reciprocally, they are said to exist contemporaneously—contemporaneousness being the existence
of what is diverse in the same time. We know
that things are in one and the same time when the
order in the synthesis of the apprehension of the
diversity is of no consequence, or when it can
proceed regularly from A, through B, C, D, E,
or, on the other hand, retrograde from E to A,
If this order in time were successive, or in the
order which begins from A and terminates in E,
it would be then impossible to begin the apprehension in the perception from E, and proceed backwards to A, because A belongs to past time, and
could no longer be an object of apprehension. If
it were assumed that in a diversity of substances
as phenomena, each thereof was entirely isolated,
that is, that no one operated upon the other, nor
partook of reciprocal influence, then contemporaneousness of the same could not be an object
of possible perception, and the existence of the
one, by no way of empirical synthesis, could
lead to the existence of the other. For if it were
fancied that these substances were separated by
means of a completely void space, the perception
which proceeds from one to the other in time,
would then determine, by means of a subsequent
perception to this other, its existence, but it could
not decide whether the phenomenon followed objectively upon the first, or rather were not one in
time with it. Through the analogy of Reciprocity,

therefore, alone can the objective contemporaneousness of objects be distinguished from the subjective succession of the same in the mind. The
apprehension of the diverse of representations
occurs at all times successively, first comes A,
then B, then C, &c. and then it must be determined
whether this is merely a contingent succession in
me—whether the succession is regularly forward
or backward, or whether these things were successive in the object,—or side by side and com-
temporaneously. This occurs only through the
understanding-conception à priori of concurrence,
which makes it general and necessary, that it is
indifferent whether the series is A, B, C, D, or D,
C, B, A, since the effect, B, not only follows upon
A, and the effect C upon B, but equally the same
occurs if the series be reversed. This necessity in
the succession when I reverse the series, causes
that I must think the things as side by side and
contemporaneous, because it does not depend upon
my will to let them follow upon one another according to an order necessarily, but I am tied
and bound to this necessity in the order when I
reverse the series, and I cognize only through the
relationship of my successive representations to an
object, in which this double succession of representations is cognized as necessary. Hence it will
be seen that the coexistence of substances in space
is the application of the category of community or
concurrence or Reciprocity between the agent and
the patient to empirical intuition. In looking at
certain objects one apprehension follows after another empirically; and I am conscious of the same
successively, but still no succession is attributed
to the objects because the apprehensions are reci-

procally related to one another. The light which
plays between our eyes and the heavenly bodies,
for instance, produces a mediate community between us and them, and thereby manifests contemporaneousness; but if the objects were separated by
void space, so that one object could not act upon
the other, it would then be impossible to say that
the objects coexist. The apprehending intellect is
the connecting link by which we remark that objects coexist, and whereby the arbitrary order of
apprehensions is represented as objectively and
universally valid.

In reflecting upon the three analogies just considered, or those into which the third category of
Relation is subdivided, we see that they are nothing else than the principles of the determination
of existence of phenomena in time, according to
all three modes of the same, namely, the relationship to time itself as a Quantity (or duration), the
relationship in time as of a Series (in succession),
and the relationship in time as a Complex of all
existences (contemporaneously). In this way we
come to the consideration of nature generally; these
analogies, in fact, being its laws. The question of
how is nature possible arises naturally from these
considerations; and we arrive at the conclusion by
an easy process, that it is the understanding
which does not derive its laws, à priori, from nature,
but presents the same to it.

Under the term Nature is meant, in the empirical
sense, the coherence of phenomena in respect of
their existence according to necessary rules or
laws; and, consequently, there must be, in this
view of the matter, certain laws à priori which
make nature possible. Only by experience and

by reason of those original laws, by virtue of which
experience itself is possible, can empirical-laws
be discovered ; and the three analogies which are
three dynamic relationships of Inherence, Consequence, and Composition, represent the unity of
nature in the connexion of all phenomena under
certain exponents, which express nothing else but
the relationship of time—so far as this comprehends
all unity in itself—to the unity of the Apperception,
which can only take place in Synthesis according
to rules. Unity of Apperception is that which
unites all the given diversity in an intuition, into
one conception of object, and consequently is the
objective.   This object must be determined in
respect of time, and this time comprehends all
existence in itself. This happens only through
conjunction or synthesis according to the three
Analogies, or laws of the Understanding just now
under consideration, whereby the object is determined as necessarily changing (accident), or as the
necessary consequence of another (effect), or as
necessarily contemporaneous with another object
(reciprocity) ; so that these three analogies of
Change, Succession, and Contemporaneousness are
the three possible relationships of time to the unity
of Apperception.

The fourth leading division of the categories has
been already stated to be that of " Modality;" and
under this are to be found the " Postulates of empirical thinking in general," and these are subdivided into three principles, and are thus stated :

Firstly, That which accords with the formal condition of experience (according to intuitions and
conceptions) is possible.

E

Secondly, that which coheres with the material conditions of experience (sensation) is real.

Thirdly, that whose coherence with the real is determined according to the general conditions of experience, is, or exists, necessarily.

These three Postulates develop the meaning of the three divisions of Possibility, Reality, and Necessity, which were before stated to be those of the category Modality, and they are so named postulates, in imitation of Geometry, where practical positions are thus denominated when they neither require nor are susceptible of demonstration. The principles of the category modality are of this description.   Modality, itself, has its seat necessarily in the understanding, and thereby an empirical object is so conjoined with the faculty of cognition, that not only is it thought with reference to the same, but also as a product of it, and the conception of modality is the conception of the way in which the representation of the object inheres in the subject of it, as thought, sensation, or law.   By the term real, we require not that a thing should be only logically possible, for every thing that does not imply contradiction is logically possible, but it also requires that the object should be given in an intuition, and that the same become thought by a category—otherwise the object would not be real.   The principle of possibility precedes our having the idea of what is, or what is not possible ; and we examine whether this principle may be conformable to the conditions of experience.   Now the difference between the principle of Possibility and Reality, which is the second postulate, is that the former only requires the formal conditions of experience, whilst the latter requires conditions which are material ; as for instance, the simple idea of an object cannot cause us to know the objective existence, or the reality of the object ; for in order to do this sensation is required, and real existence is only possible to us by means of such proof.

In the third principle, or the postulate of Necessity, we declare that whatsoever has a connexion with reality, according to the laws of experience, exists necessarily. This postulate does not imply necessity in thought merely, but also in existence. Yet effects are the only thing whose existence can positively be known. One existence is known to be necessary, as far as it refers to others, but still not of itself alone, and in this way there is no individual substance whose existence is absolutely, or rather, abstractedly necessary. It is only in relation to the effects it produces as connected with causes that this necessity can be attributed. This necessity, therefore, only regards accidents, and not substances. It is not the existence of things, (substances), but of their state whereof the necessity is cognizable by us, and this only from other states given in the perception, according to the empirical laws of causality ; and thus it follows, that the criterion of necessity alone lies in the law of possible experience.

The question of Idealism naturally arises out of this discussion, because, as the second postulate is a description of Reality, the antagonist principle of Idealism has necessarily to be refuted. Now this, as it is known, may be considered under two points of view ; one of which was adduced by Des Cartes, and the other by Berkeley. The first system may

be designated problematical Idealism, the other
dogmatical. The French philosopher declared
only one empirical assertion to be undoubted,
namely, the " I am"—the English philosopher, on
the other hand, has declared that space, with all
the things to which it adheres as inseparable condition, was impossible in itself; and consequently,
also, that the things in space were mere imagina-
tions. The latter view is inevitable, if we regard
space as a property which is to belong to things in
themselves, for then, together with all to which it
serves as a condition, it is a non-entity. But the
foundation of this idealism is destroyed if the views
adopted in the transcendental Æsthetick are admitted, and the problematical idealism of Des
Cartes only remains to be answered. This seems
easily effected by proving that it is not imagination of external things which we only possess, but
that we attain to this knowledge by experience; and
the point, therefore, is to show that even our internal, and what was to Des Cartes, indubitable
experience, is only possible by means of the external.

The Lemma here laid down is, that " the simple
but empirically determined consciousness of my
own existence, proves the existence of the objects
out of me ;" and the proof is thus adduced : Man is
conscious of his existence as determined in time.
Every determination of time presupposes something
permanent in the perception. But this permanent
cannot be an intuition in me, for all the grounds of
determination of my existence that can be met with
in me are representations, and require as such,
themselves, a permanent which is different from
them, and whereupon can be determined in rela-

tion the change thereof,—consequently my existence in the time in which they change. Against
this observation an objection may possibly be taken,
that I am not conscious of external things as things
in themselves, but as representations to which
things in themselves may lie at the foundation,
which they represent. The rejoinder to this, then,
is, I am conscious of my internal state in a determinate time, and this through internal experience.
This has reference not merely to the representations which I have, but that I may have them,
and, consequently, how in a certain determinate
time, I am existing. This would not be possible
without something out of me,—consequently the
external is not imagination; it is experience of an
external, and I come to the consciousness of the
same through the being-affected of my senses,
and not through fancy of my imagination-faculty,
by which the external is inseparably connected
with my internal sense. Provided through the
mere idea, I am, (wherein intellectual consciousness
manifests itself) I could alone be conscious of my
state, (through intellectual intuition) it would not require for internal experience necessarily the consciousness of a relationship to something out of me,
(or in the external sense). But as I am become conscious of my state, only through the being-affected
of my internal sense, and this must be permanent
in time, whilst to this something permanent must
necessarily belong—which is not to be found in the
internal sense, and consequently must be found in
the external—I am equally as conscious that there
are things out of me, or which refer to my external
sense, as I am conscious that I myself exist in time,
with certain determinations as to these or those

ideas. In this proof it will be seen that the game Idealism plays of referring every thing to internal sense, is played upon it back again by attributing all to the external one ; as only by means of it is the consciousness of our own existence possible, as determined in time,—which is, in fact, that very determined experience, or consciousness of existence, whereupon Des Cartes would make all to depend, instead of itself being dependent upon that which is external.

The categories being so far examined in detail, it becomes now advisable to make some general observations upon the system of principles as laid down, and to draw attention still more strongly to the fact, that the possibility of a thing is not to be perceived by the mere category, but that an intuition is always necessary to show the objective reality of the pure conception of the understanding. In the categories of Relation, for instance, it would be impossible to see how the division that has been laid down can be seen from mere conceptions. In no way thereby could we discover anything as to how something can exist, first only as subject, and not as mere determination of other things ; that is, can be substance—or how because something is, something else must be,—and consequently how something in general can be Cause—or how, if several things exist, because one of these exists, something follows in the others and reciprocally ; and in such manner a community of substances takes place. These, however, are all pure conceptions of the understanding, and if we proceed to the other categories, we shall find they are equally based upon the principles which have been adduced, but they are without application so long

as intuition is wanting to manifest their proof.
Without intuition it is, quite impossible to know
whether we think an object by means of the categories, or whether, in fact, any object can belong
to them ; and it is then shown that they are no
cognitions, but merely forms of thought whereby
cognitions arise, called into action by intuition. No
synthetical proposition can be made from the mere
categories, as for example, that in every existence
there is " substance," that is, that something can
exist as subject only, and not as mere predicate, or
that everything is a quantum, for in these cases
there is nothing to aid us to go out beyond a given
conception and to connect another with it ; and in
this way it will be obvious that from mere pure
conceptions of the understanding, no synthetical
proposition can be proved. Besides this—and which
is still more remarkable—it must not be overlooked,
that in order to understand the possibility of things,
and therefore to represent the objective reality of
the same, not only intuitions are required, but intuitions that are external.   For instance, if we take
the pure conceptions of Relation, we first find that
in order to give, corresponding to the conception of
substance, something permanent in the intuition,
(thereby to prove the objective result of this conception), an intuition in space (of matter) is required,
since space alone determines permanently—whilst
time, consequently, all that is in the internal sense,
flows constantly. Secondly, that in order to represent change as the corresponding intuition to
the conception of Causality, we must, for example,
take motion as change in space, and that in fact,
thereby alone can we render perceptible to ourselves changes, the possibility of which, no pure

understanding can comprehend. Change is the conjunction of contradictory opposing determinations, one to the other, in the existence of one and the same thing. Now, how it is possible, that from a given state an opposite one to it should follow of the same thing, pure reason cannot, not only without an example, render conceivable, but without an intuition, not even intelligible ; and this intuition is that of the motion of a point in space, the existence of which point in different places (as a consequence of opposite determinations) first alone makes change capable of intuition, or visible to us, for in order afterwards to render imaginable even internal changes, we make time comprehensible to ourselves, figuratively, by means of a line, as the form of the internal sense, and the internal change by means of the drawing of this line (motion)—consequently, the successive existence of ourselves in different states, by means of external intuition, the particular ground of which is this, that all change necessarily presupposes something permanent in the intuition, in order itself only to be perceived as change, though in the internal sense, no permanent intuition at all is to be met with. Lastly, the category of Community is, in respect of its possibility, not possible to be comprehended by means of mere reason, and therefore the objective reality of this conception without intuition, and this again external in space is not possible to be seen. For how can we conceive the possibility that if several substances exist, something as effect can follow, from the existence of the one to the existence of the other, reciprocally, and therefore, because there was something in the former, something must also be in the latter, which from the existence of that latter alone cannot be understood. For this is required for community, but is not at all comprehensible amongst those things where each thing is entirely isolated by means of its subsistence. Hence the final consequence is, that all principles of the pure understanding are nothing more than principles à priori of the possibility of experience, and all synthetical principles à priori relate to this last alone, nay, their possibility itself rests entirely upon such relationship.

In the observations which have hitherto been made the difference between things in themselves, or Noumena, and things as they appear, or Phenomena, has been especially alluded to, and it is the great object of the present investigation to distinguish continually these particular and opposite views. In the pure understanding, the divisions or categories have been distinctly marked out and their connexion with human intuitions exemplified, and in some degree explained. But if the enquiry were to rest here, it would appear incomplete. It seems necessary to show how from the very nature of man those errors have arisen which have thus far injured the advance of truth, and converted the science of mind into a play of logical and metaphysical subtlety and error. Now in the present instance, in his journey through the country of the pure understanding, Kant says, he has endeavoured to take into his view each portion of the land, carefully, measuring it out, and determining therein to each thing its place specifically. But then this region, to continue the metaphor, is said to be an island surrounded by a wide and stormy ocean, and the very especial seat of false or deceptive appearance, where clouds which assume the form of banks, and where masses of ice which speedily melt away, constantly delude and deceive the philosophic sailor seeking to discover new lands, and whereby he is continually led on to entertain hopes never to be realized,—hopes no sooner generated than proved to be fallacious. But if we take warning by the errors of those who have preceded us, after well examining the chart of the country clearly held in our possession, we shall find we do well to be satisfied with what we have already acquired, without grasping at more ; and we shall rather endeavour to understand and explain the principles we feel to be true, than to seek after others which surpass the bounds of human cognition.

We have seen that every thing which the understanding derives from itself, without borrowing it from experience, it still only possesses for the use of experience alone. The principles of the pure understanding, whether à priori constitutive, as the mathematical, or merely regulative, as the dynamical, contain nothing, as it were, but the pure schema only for possible experience ; for such experience has its unity simply from the synthetical unity which the understanding imparts of itself and, originally, to the synthesis of the imagination, in reference to the apperception, and to which the phenomena, as data of a possible cognition, must already stand in relation and accordance. But the understanding, it must never be forgotten, cannot make of all its principles à priori, or of its conceptions any other than an empirical, but never a transcendental use. The transcendental use of a conception in any principle is this, that it is referred to things as things in general, and to itself ; but the

empirical use is when it merely referred to phenomena, that is to objects of a possible experience.
And that the last case can only generally occur is
seen from this. To each conception is required,
first, the logical form of a conception (of thinking)
in general, and then, secondly, also the possibility
of offering an object to the conception to which it
refers. Without the object, the conception has no
sense, and is quite void of content, although it may
still always contain the logical function for forming a conception from certain data. Now the
object cannot be given to a conception otherwise
than in the intuition, and if a pure intuition is
even possible à priori before the object, such intuition still can receive its object, consequently
objective validity, only by means of the empirical
intuition, of which it is the mere form. Therefore
all conceptions and with them all principles, however much they may be possible à priori, still refer
to empirical intuitions, that is, to data of possible
experience. Without this, they have no objective
validity at all, but are a mere play either of the
imagination or the understanding respectively,
with their representations. Let us take, for example, only the conceptions of mathematics, and
first of all in their pure intuitions, " Space has
these dimensions."   " Between two points there
can be only a straight line," &c. Although all these
principles, and the representation of the object
with which this Mathematick occupies itself, are
entirely generated in the mind à priori, yet they
would mean nothing at all, could we not always
expose their meaning in phenomena (empirical objects). Consequently it is requisite also to *make
sensible* a separate conception, that is to expose the

object corresponding to it in the intuition, since without this object, the conception (so to speak) would remain without *sense*, that is, without meaning. Mathematics fulfil this condition by means of the construction of figure, which is a phenomenon present to the senses, (although produced à priori). The conception of quantity seeks even in science its support and sense, in number—and this on the fingers,—or counters of a calculating table—or in the lines and points which are exposed to our view. The conception always remains generated à priori, together with the synthetical principles or formulæ from such conceptions ; but the use of these, and reference to supposed objects, can, finally, never be sought any where but in experience, the possibility of which (according to the form) they contain à priori.

This is the case with the categories and the principles thence deduced, for we cannot make the possibility of the object of one of those to be understood, without submitting ourselves to the conditions of sensibility immediately, and consequently to the form of phenomena, in respect of which as to their sole objects, the categories must be limited. If we remove this condition, all meaning or reference to the object disappears.

No one can explain the conception of quantity in general, except in this way, that it is the determination of a thing, whereby it can be thought, how many times the number One can be placed in it. But this how many times, is founded upon successive repetition, consequently upon time, and the synthesis (of the homogeneous) therein. Reality we can only then explain in opposition to negation, provided we think a time (as the complex of all

being) which either is filled therewith, or is void.
If I omit permanence, (which is an existence in all
time,) there remains to me of the conception of
substance, nothing more than the logical representation of the subject, which I believe to realize
from this, that I represent to myself something
which can take place merely as subject, (without
being a predicate of it). But, not only, do I not
know any conditions at all under which then this
logical prerogative is proper to a thing, but there is
likewise nothing further thence to be made, and
not the least consequence to be drawn, inasmuch as
thereby no object at all of the use of this conception
is determined, and consequently we do not in fact
know whether it means any thing at all. With
respect to the conception of cause, (if I omit time,
in which something follows upon something else
according to a rule,) I should find nothing further
in the pure category than that there is something whence it may be concluded as to the existence of something else ; and thereby cause and
effect would not only not at all be able to be separated from one another, but since this capability of
conclusion still immediately requires conditions of
which I know nothing, the conception would then
have no determination as to the way it agrees with
an object. The pretended principle, "All that is contingent has a cause," presents itself certainly with
tolerable gravity, as if it had its own value in itself.
But if I ask, what do you understand by contingent? and you answer, that whose non-being is
possible, I should like to know by what you would
cognize this possibility of non-being, if you do
not represent to yourself a succession in the series
of phenomena, and in this succession an exist-

ence, which follows upon a non-existence, (or conversely)—consequently a change. For that the
non-being of a thing does not contradict itself, is a
poor appeal to a logical condition, which is certainly necessary for the conception, but which is
far from being sufficient for the real possibility,
as I then may annihilate every existing substance in thought without contradicting myself,
but cannot at all thence conclude as to the objective contingency of the same in its existence,
that is, the possibility of its non-being in itself. As
to what regards the conception of community, it
is easy to appreciate that as the pure categories
of substance as well as causality admit of no explanation determining the object, reciprocal causality in the relationship of substances to one
another (commercium) is just as little capable of it.
Possibility, Existence, Necessity, no one would be
able to explain otherwise than by a manifest tau-
tology, if we would deduce their definition singly
from the pure understanding. For the illusion of
exchanging the logical possibility of the conception
(where it does not contradict itself,) for the transcendental possibility of things, (where an object
corresponds to the conception) can only deceive and
satisfy the inexperienced.

In a word, all these conceptions are not to be
supported by means of any thing, and thereby their
real possibility demonstrated, if all sensible intuition (the only one which we have) is taken away ;
and there then only remains besides, the logical
possibility—that is, that the conception (thought) is
possible, but as to which it is not the question, but
whether the conception refers to an object, and
therefore signifies something.

Now it hence follows incontestably, that the conceptions of the pure understanding can never be of
transcendental, but at all times only of *empirical*
use, and that the principles of the pure understanding in relation to the general conditions of a
possible experience, can be referred only to objects
of the senses, but never to things in general,
(without paying regard to the manner in which we
may envisage them).

Transcendental Analytick has therefore this important result, that the understanding can never à
priori do more than anticipate the form of a possible experience in general ; and that, as that which
is not phenomenon can be no object of experience,
the understanding can never overstep the limits of
sensibility, within which alone objects are given to
us.

The pure categories, without formal conditions
of sensibility, have mere transcendental meaning,
but are of no transcendental use, since this is impossible in itself, because all conditions of any use
(in judgments) leave them, that is, the formal conditions of the subsumption of a supposed object
under these conceptions.   As, therefore, (as mere
pure categories) they are not to be of empirical
use, and cannot be of transcendental, they are of
no use at all, if we separate them from all sensibility, that is, they cannot be applied to any supposed object.   They are merely the pure form of
the use of the understanding in respect of objects
in general and of thinking, without, however, by
means of these alone our being able to determine
or think an object.

The question then now arises, since we see that
things are divided into noumena and phenomena,

whether though the pure conceptions of the understanding, or the categories are of no avail themselves, and signify nothing without they are connected with objects or phenomena, they might not have some meaning in reference to noumena, and possess some means of cognizing such. Yet this is easily answered if we pay attention to the distinction of the word noumena, when taken in a positive, and when used in a negative sense. If we understand by noumenon, a thing so far as it is an object of our sensible intuition, making abstraction of our mode of intuition of the same, this would be the negative sense. But if we understand by it, an object of nonsensible intuition, we thus assume a particular mode of intuition, namely, an intellectual one, and this would be a noumenon, in a positive sense, although this intellectual mode of intuition is not our mode, nor is it one, the possibility of which as at present constituted we can understand. If we apply categories to objects which are not considered as phenomena, we, therefore must lay at the foundation an intuition, other than a sensible one. This is, as before stated, noumenon in the positive sense, but such an intuition, namely the intellectual one, lying quite out of our faculty of cognition, the use of the categories can by no means extend beyond the limits of objects of experience, and if beings of the understanding correspond to beings of the senses, there may be, likewise, beings of the understanding to which our sensible intuition-faculty has no relation whatever. Our understanding-conceptions as mere forms of thought, do not extend in the least to these, and that therefore which is called by us noumenon, must, as such, only be understood in the negative

meaning. But if we continue the investigation a
little further, we shall arrive at another point,
which is of importance to our present enquiry, for
if I take away all thinking (or what occurs through
the categories) from an empirical cognition, it is
then found that there remains no cognition at all
of an object, for by means of mere intuition it has
been before declared and explained that nothing at
all is thought, and because such representation of
the sensibility is in me, this does not constitute any
relationship of such a representation to any object.
But if, on the contrary, I take away all intuition,
the form of thought still remains, that is, the
manner of determining an object to the diversity
of a possible intuition.   Hence the categories
extend themselves in this mode much farther than
the sensible intuition, that is, they think objects
in general, but still without looking to the particular mode (the sensibility) whereby they may
be given.   Yet do they not in this way determine a
larger sphere of objects, because we cannot admit,
that such could be given, without presupposing as
possible a kind of intuition other than a sensible
one, and yet in respect of which we are not in
the least justified. The conception of a Noumenon, however, or the conception of a thing, which
is to be thought, not at all as an object of the
senses, but as a thing in itself, by means only of a
pure understanding, is not in any degree contradictory, for we cannot assert of sensibility that
such is the only possible mode of intuition. Besides
this, the conception also is necessary not to extend
sensible intuition up to things in themselves, and
therefore to limit the objective validity of sensible
cognition.   The conception of a noumenon is,

F

therefore, strictly a limiting conception, circumscribing the pretensions of sensibility, and it is,
consequently, only of negative use, in order thereby
to show that cognition through the senses is not to
pretend to be the only possible cognition. Still
this conception is not arbitrarily imagined, but is
connected with the limitation of sensibility, yet
without being able to place any thing positive
beyond its sphere. Now, though the division of
objects, phenomena and noumena, into a sense-
world and an understanding-world, cannot be
granted in a positive signification, it is possible
to imagine an intellectual and sensible division of
conceptions. It is obvious, if we abandon the
senses, there is no mode by which we can cause
the categories to signify any thing at all, since in
order to refer to an object, something beyond the
unity of thought must be given, that is to say, an
intuition, whereupon the unity or category could
be applied. Notwithstanding this, the conception
of a noumenon, however, still remains as fixing
the sensibility within certain limits, though it is not
an intelligible object to the understanding, and we
know nothing of such understanding as that to
which it could belong, or an understanding of that
kind which cognizes its objects, not discursively
or by means of the application of the categories to
sensible intuition, but intuitively, in a non-sensible
intuition—in respect to the possibility of which we
have no idea. Our understanding receives in this
way a negative extension, inasmuch as though
limited to a certain degree by the sensibility, it on
the other hand, also itself limits the same so far
as it makes a distinction between noumena and
phenomena, and terms things in themselves by

the former title, as contra-distinguished from the latter. The expressions in modern writers of *Mundus sensibilis*, and *Mundus intelligibilis*, present a meaning so different to that in which they are used by the ancient philosophers, that some explanation becomes necessary to expose the errors which thence arise. *Mundus sensibilis*, or the world of sense, has been used to mean the complex of phenomena so far as this is envisaged or perceived, but so far as the connexion according to the general laws of the understanding is thought, it is termed *mundus intelligibilis*, or the world of the understanding. Theoretic, or rather, perhaps, it might be termed theoric or visible astronomy, which proposes the mere visual observation of the Heavens, would represent the first ; and contemplative or scientific astronomy, such as that explained by Copernicus or Newton, would represent the second. But this still would only be a perversion of words in order to avoid troublesome points, wherein each party modifies his meaning so as to meet his own views. The question at last is resolved into this, whether understanding and reason can be used, if the object submitted to them is any thing but phenomenon, for in the sense of noumenon only must it be taken if thought in itself as intelligible, or as given to the understanding alone, and not the senses. Hence, if we say that the senses represent to us the objects as they appear, but the understanding as they are, the last expression is not to be taken in a transcendental but in a mere empirical signification, namely, how they, as objects of experience, must be represented in the universal connexion of phenomena, and not according to what they may be, independent of the relation to possible experience and to the senses in general—consequently as objects of the pure understanding. The conception of mere pure intelligible objects is wholly void of all principle of application, because we cannot imagine anything as to the mode in which these are to be afforded, and the problematical idea which we have been referring to, and which as noümenon, yet leaves a place open to them, serves simply as a void space for circumscribing empirical principles, without however containing in itself, or showing any other object of cognition out of the sphere of such principles.

The Amphiboly of the conceptions of Reflection which occasion the exchange of the empirical use of the understanding for the transcendental, comes now to be considered, and this is added by Kant in the way of an Appendix, to the preceding explanation of phenomena and noumena. In order however, to make this clear, a definition and an explanation of what reflection is, necessarily precedes, and this is given in the following manner. Reflection, without which no judgment is possible, is that state of mind in which we set ourselves, in order to discover the subjective conditions under which we may attain to conceptions. It has nothing to do with the objects themselves for the purpose of obtaining conceptions of them. It is the consciousness of the relationship of given representations to our different sources of cognition, by which consciousness alone their relationship with one another can be correctly determined. The first question before any further treating of our representations is this, to what faculty of cognition do they together belong? Is it the understanding or the senses by which they are connected or compared? All judgments, that is, all comparisons, require the reflection we are now speaking of, which is a distinguishing of that cognition-faculty—that is, the understanding or the senses—to which the given conceptions belong ; and it is the action whereby I connect the comparison of representations in general with the faculty of cognition, wherein it is effected, and whereby I distinguish whether those representations are compared with one another as belonging to the pure understanding or to the sensible intuition. It is termed transcendental Reflection, the ideas being reflective. Besides this, there is another kind of reflection which is the logical Reflection, but this is only possible by means of that which is transcendental. Through the logical we only seek to know whether certain objects are identical or different, to collect those which may produce a general idea ; and as objects may be in respect of the understanding identical, and not so with regard to the sensibility, it is necessary before all logical reflection, to be certain whether the two ideas to be compared belong to the same faculty, or whether one of them does not belong to the understanding, and the other the sensibility, and in this way it is clear that it is the transcendental reflection which establishes the seat of the idea. If this distinction is not paid attention to, noumena and phenomena are confounded together, and hence arises the amphiboly of reflection, or the subject now under consideration. In this way the reflexive ideas have been placed erroneously amongst the categories, the first only serving to indicate the relationship of the given ideas, whose origin is known, whilst the last are, as has already been shown, used for the synthesis of objects.

The relationships in which conceptions to be compared can stand to one another, are the reflexive ideas of Identity and Difference, Accordance and Opposition, Internal and External, and the Determinable and the Determination (Matter and Form). The right determination of this relationship rests upon this, as to what cognition-faculty these conceptions subjectively belong to each other—whether to the sensibility or the understanding. The difference between these two last makes the difference as to the manner in which the conceptions are to be thought. With respect to identity and difference, accordance and opposition, internal and external, matter and form, Kant says, first, as to

Identity and Difference—" If an object is presented to us several times, but every time with the self-same internal determinations, (qualitas et quantitas,) it is the same thing,—if it is valid as an object of the pure understanding, it is ever the very same—and not several—but only one thing, (numerica identitas) ; but if it is phenomenon, the point is not at all then as to the comparison of conceptions, and however identical all may be in respect to the same, still the difference of the places of this phenomenon at the like time is a sufficient ground for the *numerical* difference of the object itself (of the senses). Thus in two drops of water we can entirely make abstraction of all internal difference (of quality and quantity), and it is enough that they can be perceived in different places contemporaneously, in order to hold them as numerically different. Leibnitz took phenomena for things in themselves, consequently for intelligibilia, that is, objects of the pure understanding (although on account of the confusion of their representations he gave them the name of phenomena), and then his principle of the *indistinguishable* (principium identitatis indiscernibilium) certainly could not be contested : but as they are objects of sensibility, and the understanding in respect thereof, is not of pure, but of simply empirical use, plurality and numerical difference is thus already given through space itself, as the condition of the external phenomena. For a part of space, although indeed it may be entirely similar and equal to another, is still out of it, and precisely, thereby, a part different from the first, which is added to it, in order to make up a greater space,— and thence this must hold true of all which is at the same time in the various places of space, however else such thing be similar and equal to itself.

2. *Accordance and Opposition*—" If reality is only represented to us by means of the pure understanding (realitas noumenon), no contradiction can be thought between the realities, that is, such a relationship as that these conjoined in a subject, destroy mutually one another, and 3—3, is=0. On the other hand, the real in the phenomenon (realitas phænomenon) may certainly be in opposition with one another; and united in the same subject, one annihilates *the consequence* of the other wholly, or in part, as two moving forces in the same straight line, so far as they draw or force a line in an opposite direction,—or also pleasure which holds the balance with pain.

3. The *Internal and External.*—" In an object of the pure understanding, that only is internal, which has no relation at all (according to existence) to any thing different from it. On the other hand

the internal determinations of a substantia phænomenon in space are only relationships, and it itself
(*substantia phænomenon*) wholly a complex of pure
relations. Substance in space we only know by
means of forces, which are real in this space, either
to urge others on therein (attraction), or to restrain
from forcing into it, (repulsion and impenetrability).
Other properties we do not know, which constitute the conception of substance that appears in
space, and which we name matter. Every substance, on the other hand, as object of the pure
understanding must have internal determinations
and forces, which refer to internal reality. But
what kind of internal accidents can I think to
myself, except those which my internal sense offers
to me ? namely, that which either itself is a *thinking*,
or is analogous to it. Hence Leibnitz, from all
substances, as he represented them to himself as
noumena, even from the component parts of
matter, after he had taken away in idea all that
might signify external relation, consequently *composition* also, produced simple subjects invested with
powers of representation—in a word—Monads.

4. *Matter and Form.*—" These are two conceptions which are laid at the foundation of all other
reflection, so very inseparably are they joined with
every use of the understanding. The first signifies
the determinable in general. The second, the determination of it, (both in a transcendental sense,
as we make abstraction of the difference of that
which is given, and of the manner in which it is
determined). Logicians formerly called the universal, matter, but the specific difference, form.
In each judgment we may name the given conceptions, logical matter (for judgment), their rela-

tionship, (by means of the copula) the form of the
judgment. In every being, the constituent parts
(essentialia) of it are matter, the mode in which
they are connected in a thing, the essential form.
In respect of things in general, unlimited reality
was also regarded as the matter of all possibility,
but the limitation thereof (negation) as that form,
whereby a thing distinguished itself, from another,
according to transcendental conceptions. The understanding requires, first, namely, that something
is given (at least in the conception) in order to be
able to determine it in a certain manner. Consequently matter precedes form in the conception of
the pure understanding ; and *Leibnitz* first assumes
on this account things (monads), and internally a
representation-force belonging to them, in order
afterwards to found thereupon their external relationship, and the community of their states, (that is,
of the representations.) Hence, space and time
were possible, as causes and consequences, the
first only by means of the relationship of substances,
the latter through the connexion of their determinations with one another. And so in fact would it
likewise necessarily be, if the pure understanding
could be referred immediately to objects, and if
space and time were determinations of things in
themselves. But if they are only sensible intuitions
in which we determine all objects solely as phenomena, then the form of the intuition (as a subjective quality of the sensibility) precedes all
matter, the sensations, (consequently space and
time) precede all phenomena, and all data of experience—or rather make experience first of all
possible. The intellectual philosopher could not
permit that the form would precede the things

themselves, and determine their possibility ; a censure entirely correct, if he admitted that we see
things as they are (although in confused representation). But as the sensible intuition is wholly a
particular subjective condition, which lies at the
foundation, à priori, of all perception, and the form
of which is original, the form thus of itself alone is
given, and so far from its being the case, that
matter (or the things themselves which appear)
is to lie at the foundation, (as one must judge according to mere conceptions), its own possibility
pre-supposes rather a formal intuition (time and
space) as given."

Here it will be seen that besides explaining these
ideas, the author has also another object in view,
which was to refute the theory of Leibnitz, on the
same questions, and in furtherance of this he adds,
what he terms a Scholium to the amphiboly of the
conceptions of reflection, wherein he further ex-
poses his own view of the subject. In this scholium, the place or situation which is assigned to a
conception whether in the sensibility or understanding, is characterized as the transcendental
place, and the indication, for determining this place,
for all conceptions according to rules, would be
termed transcendental Topic, or a system which
would guarantee us completely from the subrep-
tions of the pure understanding, and the delusions
thence arising, inasmuch as it at all times distinguishes to what faculty of cognition the conceptions
strictly belong.

To close finally the system of Transcendental
Analytick, the table of the division of the con-
ception of *Nothing* is introduced as opposed to
Something, and as the categories are the only con-

ceptions which refer to objects in general, the distinction of an object whether it is *something* or *nothing* proceeds according to the order and directions of the categories.*

NOTHING.

as

1.

VOID CONCEPTIONS WITHOUT OBJECT:—Ens rationis.

2.

VOID OBJECT OF A CONCEPTION:—Nihil privativum.

3.

VOID INTUITION WITHOUT OBJECT :—Ens imaginarium.

4.

VOID OBJECT WITHOUT CONCEPTION :—Nihil negativum.

Here terminates one of the most important divisions of the critical philosophy. The first part of the work, as we have seen, is termed transcendental Elemental Doctrine, and is composed of the two great divisions of transcendental Æsthetick and transcendental Logic. The first of these, or transcendental Æsthetick, is only concerned with the explanation of space and time ; the second, or transcendental Logic, enters into the subject generally, whether general or transcendental ; and under each of these divisions, whether denominated simply as Analytick and Dialectick, or transcen-

---

* Kant proved himself the umpire between Sensuality and Intellect. Until his time, ever since that of Des Cartes, it had been a subject of bitter dispute, whether philosophical knowledge or conceptions were, as according to the Sensualists, derived from experience, or, as according to the Intellectualists, from pure Reason. Kant demonstrated that all phenomenal knowledge must arise from the cooperation of the outward and the inward. An intellect that loses sight of experience, has no object on which to act. The objects which experience presents to us, cannot truly be said to exist until Intellect, with its arranging and combining power, commences its operation upon them.—*See Foreign Quarterly Review*, 98.

dental Analytick and transcendental Dialectick, the whole faculty of the understanding becomes dissected and explained with reference to the categories, their schematism, and to judgments. The synthetical principles also of the pure understanding, when more fully explained, are shown to be Axioms of Intuition, Anticipations of Perception, and Analogies of Experience, whether regarded as Principles of the permanence of substance of Succession, or of Coexistence, and Postulates of empirical Thinking in general.

To this development of the qualities of the Intelligence, another division has been added, showing the grounds of the distinction of all objects in general into Phenomena and Noumena—and lastly, an explanation is subjoined of the Amphiboly that arises from exchanging the empirical use of the understanding for the transcendental. This leads naturally to the second great division of Logic, or that which is to be treated of in a succeeding part, under the title of Transcendental Dialectick.

Before entering however upon this new subject, it may not be useless to recapitulate succinctly those principles which we have had under consideration and the connexion existing between them ; and if any thing further should still be required for the more complete understanding of the doctrines of the critical Philosophy than is to be found in the " Critick," reference must be made to the " Prolegomena," where the writer's views are still more developed, and to the " Logic " where questions appertaining to this subject particularly are explained at length, and where they are perhaps more systematically handled than in the work now under analysis. In the particular work before us, however, most of the questions as to the logical use of the Understanding in general are discussed at considerable length; and the application of those laws which regulate that operation of mind which is denominated thinking, are most especially considered.

This operation is shown to be an act wherein we represent objects to ourselves, by adding certain designations to them. The representation is termed a conception, whilst the designations are predicates of the object itself. Logic as a science is found to be universal and particular, and the first is divided into pure and applied. In pure we abstract all the empirical conditions under which the understanding is exercised. The science is called applied when it is directed towards the rules of the understanding-use, under those subjective empirical conditions which Psychology teaches. Universal Logic contains the absolutely necessary rules of thinking; whilst particular Logic contains the rules of thinking correctly in a certain sort of objects. Applied Logic consequently, as a branch of this, treats of attention, of whatever hinders or promotes it, of the origin of error, illusion, prejudices, &c. Pure Logic is divided into the doctrines of the understanding, of judgment and of reason, or the doctrines of conceptions, judgments, and syllogisms. The Understanding possesses conceptions as so many rules for the thinking of objects; but it is not the design of the Science under consideration, to enquire after the origin of these. Judgment is the placing of objects under these rules. A syllogism is the deduction of one judgment from another. If we separate the designations, by the addition of which we represent an object to ourselves, in the object, that which we retain in thought, divested of its designations, is the analytical unity of consciousness, and it forms the basis of all conceptions or of all thinking.

In all judgments, conjunction and agnition are to be distinguished from one another; the first consists in the transition of consciousness from one conception to the other, so that both come to one consciousness, but agnition consists in the placing of an object under a precise conception. The original use of the understanding, (it cannot be too often repeated,) consists of the categories, and their exhibition as postulates is that same original use, and this is seen to consist every where in original composition or synthesis, and in original agnition or schematism. Transcendental Philosophy is the science of the original use of the understanding in the categories.—Critical idealism consists in the position that the understanding conjoins originally in the categories; and that the use of the categories as predicates of objects, (that is to say, the conjunction we place in the things), entirely rests on the original intellectual conjunction. Synthetic unity and analytical unity seem in the first instance embarrassing, because they appear to run into one another, but duly considered, a marked distinction is shown to exist between them, though from the corresponding nature of their functions to separate faculties of the mind, they are frequently confounded. In an analytical judgment those designations are added to a thing, which are already thought in the conception of this thing, and whereby the analytical unity of this conception is first fixed. Now it has been shown that this analytical unity is the basis of all conceptions,

or of all thinking, and the analytical unity of consciousness is the simple point we retain in
thought in reference to an object, when we have
separated the designations by whose addition we
represent any object to ourselves. Synthetic unity
conjoins the different representations in every intuition ;   and as it refers to the understanding, it
may, so far only as it merely renders possible the
various ways of uniting the given diverse or multiplex though intuition, be termed the pure conception of the understanding. The supreme unity
thereof is that whereby every compounded cognition is thought as something, or as an object; and
we have seen that the number of these pure synthetic unities or categories is twelve. The synthetic unity is opposed to the analytic. With the
farther developement of these principles, but preceded by a full explanation on the doctrines of
time and space which form the basis of the Kantian
philosophy, and wherein it is assumed that these
qualities are only forms of thought and not anything in themselves, the first great division of the
subject is concluded, and the attention is afterwards
directed to the application and proof of the positions, rather than to any further elucidation of the
nature and quality of the human mind.

TRANSCENDENTAL DIALECTICK.

In alluding to the subject of Dialectick in general, it is termed in the earlier part of the work,
" Logic of Appearance," but by this expression it
was not intended to convey that this has any thing
to do with appearance in the sense of phenomenon ;

but that it concerns the errors of false appearance, and explains the causes which lead to this, and which gives rise to so many erroneous conclusions. It has been already shown that there are only two sources of cognition, the understanding and the senses ; and consequently the errors now to be exhibited arise from an unobserved influence of the latter upon the former, whence it occurs that the subjective grounds of judgment confound themselves with the objective, and cause such to deviate from their destination, for sensitivity, subjected to the operation of the understanding, is the source of real cognition. But this same sensitivity, so far as it influences the action of the understanding itself, and determines it for judgments, is the foundation of error : for in the senses there is no judgment at all : neither true nor false.

In order to distinguish the particular action of the one from the force of the other which is mixed up with it, it is necessary to look upon erroneous judgment, therefore, as the diagonal between two forces, which determines the judgment according to two different directions ; and to resolve the compound effect in question, into the simple one of the understanding and the sensibility, and this is effected by transcendental reflection. Here it becomes necessary to refer to the distinction between the terms Transcendent and Transcendental, in order to obviate any confusion that may hereafter arise. The knowledge that a certain intuition, conception, or principle refers à priori to objects of experience, inasmuch as it is by these, that experience is rendered possible, is denominated transcendental ; but as the categories can never outstep empirical intuition, nor can ever be otherwise than of empirical use; whenever a principle pretends to pass these limits, it is called transcendent: a principle may also be termed immanent, when by means of our investigation of pure reason, we have been enabled to succeed so far as to expose the illusion or false appearance of the pretended transcendent principles and to deprive them of their claim to being considered as objective judgments.

Logical appearance or illusion, that is, the appearance of conclusions false in themselves, consists in a mere imitation of the form of reason, and the illusion soon disappears, attention being paid to the case; but transcendental appearance or illusion does not in the same way cease, although it may have been fully exposed and its nothingness shown. The cause of this is, that in reason considered subjectively as a human faculty of cognition, fundamental rules lie which have completely the air of objective principles—whereby it occurs that the subjective necessity of a certain connexion between our conceptions in favour of the understanding is reckoned as an objective necessity of the determination of things in themselves. This illusion is, it is obvious, no more to be avoided than it is in our power to prevent the sea from ~~not~~ appearing more elevated in the middle than when near the shore; nor the moon from seeming to be largest when rising from the horizon, although no deception is practised upon the scientific observer by either one or other of these appearances.

The object of Transcendental Dialectick then will be to exhibit the illusions of transcendental judgments. But that these illusions should thereby cease, as they do in Logic when attention is awakened, cannot result from any study of the subject ; for in the cases to be investigated it will be seen that we have continually to do with, not only a natural but an unavoidable appearance or illusion, which though it reposes upon subjective principles, constantly substitutes them for objective, whereas Logical Dialectick has only to correct errors in the following up of principles. Trans- cendental Dialectick necessarily and unseparably adheres to human reason, and even when its de- lusions are discovered they perpetually recur and lead us into difficulty.

In treating of Reason, the first question which naturally presents itself is, what is reason ? and here another difficulty immediately springs up, because if reason be denominated " the Faculty of principles," which it undoubtedly is, the expression is ambiguous, the word principle, commonly, only signifying a cognition which may certainly be used as a principle, although in fact in itself, and accord- ing to its proper origin, it is no principle in the sense now to be adopted. For instance, every general proposition, even although it may be derived from experience, (by induction), can serve as a major in a syllogism, but it is not on that account itself a prin- ciple. Mathematical axioms (for example, " there can only be a straight line between two points") are indeed in general cognitions à priori, and therefore with propriety are termed principles re- latively to the cases which can be subsumed under them. But still on this account I cannot say that I know the property of the straight line in general and in itself, from principles, but only in the pure intuition.

Cognition from principles may be termed, therefore, that where the particular is cognized in the general by means of conceptions. Every syllogism is thus a form of the deduction of a cognition from a principle. For the major always furnishes a conception, which causes that all which is subsumed under the condition of it, is known from it, according to a principle. Now as every general cognition can serve as a major in a syllogism, and the understanding furnishes such general propositions à priori, these also in respect to their possible use, may thus be termed principles.

But if we consider these principles of the pure understanding in themselves, according to their origin, they are any thing but cognitions from conceptions. For they would not even be once possible at all à priori, did we not hereby draw in pure intuition (in mathematics), or the conditions of a possible experience in general. That all which happens has a cause, cannot at all be concluded from the conception of that which happens generally. The principle rather shows how we first of all can acquire from that which happens, a determinate experience-conception.

The understanding therefore cannot procure synthetical cognitions from conceptions, and it is these properly, which absolutely are termed principles, inasmuch as all universal propositions in general may be termed comparative principles.

It is a very old wish, says Kant, and one which, who knows how late, may perhaps sometime be accomplished, that, for once, instead of the endless variety of civil laws, we might investigate their principles, for therein alone consists the secret of simplifying Legislation, so called. But the laws are here still only limitations of our liberty upon conditions under which it continually accords with itself—consequently they refer to something, which is entirely our own work, and whereof we, through the conceptions in question, ourselves may be the cause. But how objects in themselves—how the nature of things stands under principles, and is to be determined according to mere conceptions,—is, if not something impossible, still at least very strange. But however this may be, (for the enquiry respecting it remains yet to be made), it at least thence is evident, that cognition from principles (in themselves) is something quite other than mere understanding-cognition, which certainly indeed may precede other cognitions in the form of a principle, but in itself, (so far as it is synthetical,) does not rest upon mere thinking, nor contain in itself something general, according to conceptions.

The understanding may be a faculty of the unity of phenomena by means of rules ; and reason is thus the faculty of the unity of the rules of the understanding under principles. Reason, therefore, never refers directly to experience, or to an object, but to the understanding, in order to give to the diverse cognitions of this, unity à priori by means of conceptions, which may be termed unity of reason, and which is of quite another kind to that which can be derived from the understanding.

Reason in its logical use is the faculty of concluding *mediately* or the faculty of deducing one judgment from another, by means of an intermediate judgment, and such a conclusion is termed a reason-conclusion, to distinguish it from an understanding-conclusion, wherein the truth of one judgment follows upon another *immediately*, without requiring a third.

In every syllogism, a rule is first thought (this is the major), by means of the understanding. Secondly, a cognition is subsumed under the condition of the rule, (this is the minor) by means of the faculty of judgment. Lastly is determined cognition by means of the predicate of the rule, (this is the conclusion), and consequently à priori by reason. That relationship therefore which the major represents as the rule between a cognition and its condition, makes up all the different kinds of syllogisms ; and as all judgments are three-fold in relationship according to the table, there are also the same number and classes of syllogisms, or, there are the categorical, hypothetical, and disjunctive. Reason in fact is that faculty which may be termed the third and highest degree of mental spontaneity, and its action consists, like that of the intellect or understanding, in connecting a variety ; and in its conclusions it always endeavours to reduce the great diversity of the cognition of the understanding, to the smallest number of principles or general conditions, and thereby to effect the greatest unity of the same.

The pure use of reason next comes here to be considered, that is to say, can we isolate reason ? and is it then still a peculiar source of conceptions and judgments which spring up only out of it, whereby it refers to objects, or is it a mere subaltern faculty for giving a certain form to given cognitions, which is called logical, through which the cognitions of the understanding only are subjected one to another, and inferior rules to others which are higher, the condition of one embracing that of the other in its sphere ? These questions may be still more shortly expressed in the enquiry whether reason in itself or pure reason à priori contains synthetical principles and rules, and if it does, wherein do these principles consist ? The reply to this must be sought for in the formal and logical procedure of the same reason in syllogisms, wherein it is observable that syllogisms do not apply to intuitions but to conceptions, so that the unity of reason is not the unity of a probable experience, but essentially different from it ; and the general condition of a judgment of reason or conclusion in a syllogism, is nothing else but a judgment, by means of the subsumption of a condition under a general rule. As this rule is again subjected to the same proofs of reason, and the condition of the condition must be sought after as long as we can, it is manifest that the especial principle of reason in general, or in the logical use, is to find for the conditioned cognitions of the understanding, the Unconditioned or absolute, whereby the unity of the whole is to be completed.

Now as this logical maxim cannot be otherwise a principle of pure reason, excepting it is thereby admitted, that if the conditioned be given, the whole series of conditions subjected one to another, is likewise then given, (and which series itself is therefore unconditioned), and as such a principle is evidently synthetical and not analytical, (the condition referring always to a previous condition but never to the unconditioned), there must arise from this, other different synthetical propositions of which the understanding can know nothing, since, as it has been over and over again repeated, it has nothing to do but with objects of experience, and certainly the unconditioned is not one of these. Hence, in reference to the highest principle of pure reason, such other principles as are connected with it must be transcendent, no empirical use being to be made of them ; whilst the principles of the understanding are on their part immanent, because they only concern objects of experience. The question as to the principle under consideration, that is to say, whether the principle has objective truth or not, that the series of conditions, (in the synthesis of phenomena or of the thinking of things in general), reaches or does not reach to the unconditioned—and what consequences thence result to the empirical use of the understanding—or in other words— whether there is such an objectively valid proposition of reason at all, or merely a logical precept in rising from higher and higher conditions to approach to the completeness of the same, and thereby to bring the highest unity of reason possible to us into one cognition, whether, in fact, this requirement of reason has been held to be a transcendental principle of pure reason,—this is the object of the Transcendental Dialectick, now under investigation. To ascertain this, the transcendental conceptions of pure reason are first to be treated of, and subsequently those syllogisms which are transcendental and dialectical.

The conceptions of pure reason differ from those then of the understanding very materially. The former are not limited in their experience, because they regard cognitions whereof every empirical one only contains a part, and to the extent of which, no real experience ever extends, though always belonging to it. Now, though conceptions of the understanding are thought à priori, before experience, and in its favour, they contain nothing more than the unity of phenomena, so far as these

belong necessarily to a possible empirical consciousness. They first afford matter for conclusion, and no conceptions à priori of objects precede them from which they could be concluded.
Their objective reality, it cannot be too often repeated, rests upon this, that whilst they constitute
the intellectual form of all experience, their application must at all times be able to be shown in
experience. Now conceptions of reason appear
in the same light for the comprehending, as
conceptions of the understanding do, for the understanding of perceptions, and if they contain the
unconditioned, they then concern something to
which all experience certainly belongs, but which
itself is never an object of experience,—something
indeed towards which reason leads in its conclusions
from experience, but which never forms a member
of the empirical synthesis.

In considering the mode in which the term Idea
was employed by Plato, it seems very much to
answer to that conception of Pure Reason now
adopted. This distinguished philosopher made use
of the word in such a way as to give it to be understood, that he thereby meant something which not
only is never derived from the senses, but which
even rises above the conceptions of the understanding, and concerning which object Aristotle
was especially occupied, since in experience itself
never anything agreeing with idea is to be found. In
Plato's view, ideas are the archetypes of things themselves, and not, like the categories, keys to possible
experience, Idea, therefore, in the observations
that are to follow, must be carefully distinguished
from all other terms, and the scale recommended
by Kant is the following. The class is represen-

tation in general. Under it stands the representation with consciousness (perceptio). A perception which refers only to the subject, as the
modification of its state, is sensation (sensatio).
An objective perception, is cognition (cognitio),
and this is either intuition or conception (intuitus
vel conceptus). The former refers immediately to
the object, and is single ; the latter mediately, by
means of a mark which may be common to several
things. The conception is either an empirical or
pure conception ; and the pure conception, so far
as it has only its origin in the understanding, (not
in the pure image of the sensibility,) is called
notio. A conception from notions, which over-
steps the possibility of experience, is the idea or
the conception of reason. To one who has once
been accustomed to this distinction, it must be in-
tolerable to hear the representation of the colour
red termed idea. It is not even to be called notion
or conception of the understanding.

Having in some degree then explained the meaning of the term idea, the next point that engages
the attention is that in reference to transcendental
Ideas. Ideas themselves have been shown to be conceptions of reason, and to be quite distinct from
conceptions of the understanding, through which,
as it has been stated, the connexion of the variety in
an empirical intuition is thought as an object, or
as being universally valid for every body. These categories, however, are not derived from conclusions,
nor do they presuppose any other conceptions,
from which they may be deduced. They render
phenomena intelligible by giving objective and
universal validity to our empirical intuitions. Every
conclusion, it is true, that ascends to the Uncon-

ditioned must begin from the categories, because only by them can what is given be thought as conditioned, or as an object ; but on the other hand, those conceptions of reason by which the unconditioned is thought, are Ideas.

In the former part of the work, or in transcendental Analytick, the categories were deduced from the Forms of judgments, and from the completed developement of these, we seek those conceptions which constitute the foundation of the objective unity of consciousness in general. Now as the form of Judgments (changed into a conception of the synthesis of intuitions) produces the categories, just in the like way we may expect that the Form of syllogisms, if we apply this to the synthetical unity of intuitions, in pursuance with the categories, will contain the origin of particular conceptions à priori, and which may be termed also, pure conceptions of the understanding, or transcendental ideas.

The word idea is used in the sense of a necessary conception of reason to which no congruous object in the senses can be given, and the pure conceptions of reason are transcendental ideas. They are pure conceptions of pure reason, inasmuch as they consider all experience-cognition, as determined through an absolute unity of conditions. The word absolute is taken here in that extended signification which critical philosophy carefully attaches to it. The pure reason-conceptions are not arbitrarily imagined, but they are transcendent, and overstep the limits of all experience.

The function of reason in its conclusions consists in the Generality of the cognition according to conceptions ; and syllogism itself is a judgment

which is à priori determined in the whole extent
of its condition. For instance, the position that
" Caius is mortal," might be derived from experience simply by means of the understanding ;
but a conception is sought for which contains the
condition, under which the predicate or assertion in
general of this judgment is given. In this case
the general conception is man, and when it is subsumed under the condition taken in its whole extent, that " Man is mortal," it is determined that
" Caius is mortal."

In following up the same mode of proceeding with
respect to reason that we did with regard to the
understanding in looking at the deduction of the
categories, we may discover that reason possesses
a synthetical principle à priori, for it is evident that
its logical operation is to seek absolute condition in
a synthesis of cognitions, and there to produce the
greatest systematic unity. Reason, in fact, seeks
the absolute condition whereupon depend the conditional cognitions of the understanding, and
whence results the synthetical principle à priori,
whereof reason continually makes use, that is to
say—that when the conditional is given, all the conditions without exception are given with it, and
consequently the Absolute itself is given. This idea
is synthetical, for the idea of the conditional comprehends that of the condition, but not that of the
Absolute. As it has been shown that there are
three forms of judgments in the category of Relation, there will be consequently three kinds of ideas
with respect to the Absolute, and there can only be
these three ideas, the categories of Quantity and
Quality, not entering into the synthesis of the subject with the predicate as connected with one

another, but only individually. Neither does the
category of Modality enter into our consideration.
It does not contribute in any way to the synthesis
of the two ideas. These only concern the Reality
or the Necessity of the predicate,—the subject
always remaining conditional—and the categories
of Relation therefore are those only which furnish
Ideas of reason, and reason is only satisfied when
it has concentrated in the Absolute every thing
that the understanding has furnished which is conditional or individual. There can be only three
kinds of dialectical conclusions that refer to triple
modes of conclusion, and by means of which
reason can reach from principles to cognitions.
In every thing the business of reason is to ascend
from that conditioned synthesis to which the understanding at all times remains tied, to the unconditioned which the understanding can never attain.

The General in all relationship which our representation can have, is first, reference to the subject ;
secondly, reference to objects, either indeed as phenomena, that is, objects of intuition, or as objects
of thought generally ; and connecting this sub-
division with the one that has preceded, all relationship of representations, whereof we either make
to ourselves a conception or an idea, is threefold,
the relationship to the subject—to the diverse of
the object in the phenomena—and to all things in
general.

Now, all pure conceptions in general have to do
with the synthetical unity of representations ; but
conceptions of pure reason (transcendental ideas)
with the unconditioned synthetical unity of all conditions in general. Consequently all transcendental ideas may be brought under three classes of

which the first contains the absolute (unconditioned) unity of the thinking subject; the second, the absolute unity of the series of the conditions of the phenomenon ; the third, the absolute unity of the condition of all objects of thought in general.

The thinking subject is the object of Psychology ; the complex of all the phenomena (the world) is the object of Cosmology; and the thing which contains the supreme condition of the possibility of every thing that can be thought (the essence of all essences), is the object of all Theology. Consequently, pure reason furnishes the idea of a transcendental doctrine of the soul (Psycologia rationalis), of a transcendental science of the world (Cosmologia rationalis), and finally also of a transcendental cognition of God (Theologia transcendentalis).

More than these three transcendental ideas there cannot be, and as reason, in order to arrive at them, begins its ascent from the conditioned synthetic unity, that is, from objects of intuition, they will proceed according to the order of the categories. For pure reason never refers directly to objects, but to the conceptions of the understanding in respect of them. No objective deduction of the transcendental ideas now under consideration is strictly possible, because they have no relation to an object, that could congruously be given to them, because they are only ideas, and no objective validity to any given object can be shown. Hitherto this only has been gained, that these transcendental conceptions of reason have been withdrawn from the equivocal position which they held in the systems of certain philosophers, and they have been entirely separated from the conceptions of the understanding, whilst at the same time their number has been fixed, and their origin has been determined.*

In referring once more to the dialectical conclusions of Pure Reason, and before investigating the table of the same in the order prescribed, it is important again to repeat, that in speaking as to an object whose real possibility we cannot represent to ourselves, we commonly say we have no conception of it, and we may state the same thing with respect to transcendental ideas, because as no intuition corresponds to them, we can have no conception thereof; but we should express ourselves better upon this point, if instead of the expression in its simple sense, it was qualified by saying we can have no acquaintance with the object corresponding to such an idea, but that we have a problematical conception of it.

Having explained the nature of Reason, and the impossibility of attaining to any knowledge of it empirically, the next division of the subject con-

---

* Metaphysick has for the particular object of its enquiry only three ideas, God, Freedom, and Immortality, in such a way, that the second conception conjoined with the first, must lead to the third as a necessary consequence. Every thing with which this Science otherwise occupies itself, serves it simply as a means for the purpose of arriving at these Ideas and their reality. It does not require them in favour of the science of nature, but in order to issue out beyond nature. The insight into the same would render Theology, Morals, and by the junction of both, Religion, consequently the highest objects of our existence, dependent merely upon the speculative faculty of reason, and nothing else. In a systematic representation of such ideas, this stated order, as the synthetical one, would be the most suitable; but in the investigation which must necessarily precede it, the analytical which inverses this order would be more adapted to the end, to enable us, (since we proceed from that which experience immediately furnishes us, from Psychology, to Cosmology, and thence to the cognition of God,) to complete our great design.

ducts us to the description and analysis of these dialectical syllogisms, which lead to error, and cause us to attribute objective reality to that which in fact is only subjective.

The transcendental (subjective) reality of the pure conceptions of reason rests at least upon this, that we are brought by means of a necessary conclusion of reason or syllogism to such Ideas. There are, consequently, conclusions of reason which contain no empirical premises, and by means of which we conclude from something that we know, as to something else whereof we yet can have no conception, and to which, notwithstanding, by means of an unavoidable appearance, we grant objective reality. Such conclusions in respect of their result, are, consequently, rather to be termed sophistical than rational conclusions, although on account of the occasion of them, they may well assume the latter term, because they are not wholly fictitious, nor have they sprung up accidentally, but have arisen out of the nature of reason. They are sophistications not of men, but of pure reason itself, from which the wisest of mankind cannot free himself, and although perhaps after much trouble, indeed, he may avoid error, yet can he never be rid of that false appearance which continually torments and sports with him.

These dialectical syllogisms are, as has already been mentioned, of three kinds, the categorical, the hypothetical, and the disjunctive. The first may be termed the Paralogism of Pure Reason, the second the Antinomy of Pure Reason, and the third the Ideal of Pure Reason.

Now logical paralogism consists in the erroneousness of a syllogism according to form, but transcendental paralogism differs from this that in having a transcendental foundation, it concludes falsely according to form. In this way a false conclusion will have its foundation in the very nature of human reason, and carry along with it an inevitable illusion, and one which at the same time is insoluble. In the earlier part of this Analysis, the originally synthetic unity of Apperception or the " I think" was shortly alluded to. The farther explanation naturally arises here, and the sense in which the I is to be looked upon, critically speaking, will be rendered more intelligible. The doctrines of rational Psychology itself are founded upon the errors which spring up in the consideration of the " I think," and in not separating what is pure from all that is empirical, whereby the character of a rational science is destroyed, and an empirical one is continually substituted. Rational psychology is founded upon these four propositions, according to the order of the categories, first in regard to relation, that the same is substance—in regard to quality, that it is simple—in regard to quantity, that it is one—in respect of the different times in which it exists, it is numerically identical, that is, is unity, and not plurality—and fourthly, in respect to modality, that it stands in relationship to all possible objects in space. From these elements arise all conceptions of pure psychology, but solely by means of combination. The substance in question, merely as object of internal sense, furnishes the conception of immateriality; as simple substance, of incorruptibility; its identity, as intellectual substance, gives personality; and all these then taken together, spirituality. The relationship to objects in space gives commercium with bodies,—consequently it represents the thinking-substance as the principle of life in matter, or as soul, and as the foundation of animality. This limited by spirituality gives immortality. All rational Psychology is thus built upon the I. But of this I, isolated, we cannot have the least conception, independently of a representation, for we are only conscious of the I, in the " I think," and this so far only as something is thought, and we turn round about as it were in a continual circle, because we are always compelled to make use of its representation, in order to judge something in respect of itself; that is, we are obliged to use its representation in representing it. Now, in investigating minutely the question of the substantiality of the soul, we shall find that it rests upon the proposition that whatever is the absolute subject of our judgments, and which, consequently, cannot be employed as predicate, is Substance. I, as thinking subject, am the absolute subject of all my judgments, and I cannot be the predicate of another object; then, as thinking subject, I am Substance.

Now this reasoning is a Paralogism, and is one of those fallacies which it is the especial object of the " Critick" to expose and detect ; and it will be seen, in considering this question further, that there is nothing gained, by means of the analysis of the consciousness of myself in thinking in general, in respect of the cognition of myself, as Object, but that the logical exposition of thinking in general is erroneously held to be a metaphysical determination of the object.

The objective reality of the category substance in empirical intuitions has been previously shown,

H

in the Deduction of the principles of transcendental
judgment; but to the representation I, no intuition
corresponds, because it merely expresses the act of
consciousness, and has only signification in the
connexion of representations; and hence that the
I, as an existing thing, can exist only as subject,
that is, I am substance, is far more than can be
found in the mere conception of thinking. That
the I in all thinking in fact can occur only as subject, but never as predicate, is an apodictical
position, because it is identical; for this is merely
the exposition of the conception of thinking,
but it does not mean that I, as object of myself,
am a self subsisting being or substance. Secondly,
the I in each apperception or thinking is singular,
and cannot be resolved into a plurality of subjects.
This lies in the conception of Thinking, and it is
an analytical proposition, but it does not mean
that the thinking I is a simple substance, because
this would not be an analytical, but a synthetical
proposition. The conception of substance refers
always to intuitions, which can never be anything
but sensible in me, and lie therefore entirely out of
the field of the understanding and its thinking, yet
in respect of which, we pretend to speak when we
say, that the I in thinking is simple. Thirdly,
the proposition of the identity of myself in all
the diversity of which I am conscious, is equally
an analytical proposition, but this identity of the
subject, whereof I can be conscious in all its representations, does not concern the intuition of
this subject by which it is given as object. To
represent the I, as substance, always the same
for an intuition, it is necessary to represent it as
substance. Fourthly and lastly, it is an analytical

proposition, when I separate my own existence, as that of a thinking being, from that of other things external to me.   But to say that I exist as a substance, different from external things, it is not the same thing, and it is a synthetical proposition.   In fact, whether this consciousness of myself, without things external to me, and whereby representations are given to me, be possible, and whether, therefore, I can exist simply as thinking being, that is, without being what I am, man, I do not thereby know, nor does the analysis of consciousness in the conception of thinking, at all assist me, when, by means of the conception I, it is attempted to determine this I as an object, because this necessarily requires intuition, without which, no synthetical position, it has been already remarked, is possible.

All this is made more clear by reference to what has gone before in the explanation of the principles of transcendental judgment, where if attention is paid to the scholium, attached to the general representation of principles and to the observations upon noumena, it is shown, that the conception of a thing that can exist of itself as subject, but not as mere predicate, still carries along with it no objective reality at all ;   that is, we cannot know whether an object at all can belong to it, since we do not perceive the possibility of such a mode of existing ; and consequently this can give absolutely no cognition.   If therefore we have to denote under the denomination of a substance, an object which can be given—if this is to become a cognition—then a permanent intuition, as the indispensable condition of the objective reality of a conception, namely, that whereby alone the object is given—must be laid at the foundation. But we have in the internal intuition in question nothing permanent, for the I is only the consciousness of my thinking; and consequently there is wanting, if we stop short simply at thinking, the necessary condition for applying the conception of substance, that is, of a self-subsisting subject, to itself as thinking being; and the therewith conjoined simplicity of substance entirely falls away, together with the objective reality of the conception, and it becomes changed into a mere logical qualitative unity of self-consciousness in thinking in general, whether the subject be composed or not.

In the simple nature of the soul, the immortality thereof was at one time supposed to be proved, but Mendelsohn soon perceived that though, if we admit it to be a simple being, it cannot cease by means of division, yet something further would be wanting to secure to it a necessary continuance, inasmuch as a cessation of its existence might equally as well be conceived by its vanishing away, as if it took place by division. In his Phædo, he sought to guard against this annihilation by showing that a simple being cannot cease to be, because it cannot be at all diminished, and thereby lose something step by step of its existence, and so by degrees be changed into nothing. Having no parts it has no plurality in itself, and if it were to cease to be entirely,—between one moment wherein it is, and another wherein it is not,—a time must elapse. But as it is evident we may also say, no time has elapsed, because the same moment which belongs to its existence belongs to its non-existence, such a contradiction, in adopting the principle of the

vanishing of the soul, led to a supposition in the
mind of Mendelsohn of its perdurability or permanence. But he did not well consider that although
we accord to the soul this simple nature and that it
contains no extensive quantity, we cannot refuse
to it intensive quantity—that is to say, such a
degree of reality as may decrease through all
infinitely smaller degrees; and that thus the pretended substance may still be changed into nothing,
although not through division, but through that
gradual diminution, which it was wished to obviate.
For consciousness has always a degree which may
ever be diminished, and in the elanguescence of
consciousness that of the soul would be implied.
If from the transcendental expression, " I am "
we refer the existence of the soul, as substance independent of external objects, then idealism, or at
least problematical idealism is unavoidable.

If we take the foregoing propositions in synthetical connexion, and as they must be taken as valid
for all thinking beings in rational Psychology as a
system, and if we proceed from the category of relation in the proposition, " all thinking beings are
as such substances," through the series thereof
backwards, until the circle is concluded, we thus
stumble at last upon that existence, of which they
themselves, (the thinking beings), in this system, independent of external things, are not only conscious, but are also able from themselves, in respect of the permanence which necessarily belongs
to the character of substance, to determine such.

If we follow, on the other hand, the analytical
procedure,—because the " I think" is a proposition,
which already includes within itself an existence

as given, — (consequently modality lies at the foundation)—and if we analyze this proposition in order to cognize its content, namely, whether and how this I in space or time thereby simply determines its existence ;—the propositions of rational psychology would then begin not from the conception of a thinking being in general, but from a reality : and from the manner in which this is thought, after all that is empirical with respect to it has been separated, that which belongs to a thinking being in general will be deduced, as the following table shows:—

1.

I think.

2. As subject. 3. As simple subject.

4. As identical subject in each state of my thinking.

Now since in the second proposition it is not determined, whether I can exist and be thought only as subject, and not also as predicate of another, the conception of a subject is thus taken in this case merely logically, and it remains undetermined whether substance is to be understood or not under this. But in the third proposition, the absolute unity of the apperception, the simple I in the representation, whereunto all conjunction or separation that constitutes the thinking refers, is also important in itself, although I have not yet decided any thing as to the quality or subsistence of the subject. The apperception is something real, and its simplicity already lies in its possibility. Now in space nothing is real which is simple, for points, (which constitute the only simple thing in space,) are merely limits, but never even any thing that serves to constitute space as a part. Consequently there follows from this, the impossibility of an explanation of my quality, as mere thinking subject, from principles of materialism. But since my existence in the first proposition is considered as given, since it does not say every thinking being exists, (which at the same time would state absolute necessity), and therefore state too much respecting these beings ; but only, I *exist* thinking, it is thus empirical, and contains the determinateness of my existence, merely in respect of my representations in time. But as I again, for this, first, require something permanent, and such, so far as I think myself, is not at all given to me in the internal intuition, the manner in which then I exist, whether as substance or accident, it is not at all possible to determine by means of this simple self-consciousness. Consequently, if materialism is incomplete as a mode of explanation of my existence, so is spiritualism just equally insufficient, and the conclusion is, that we cannot in any way, whatever it may be, cognize any thing as to the quality of our souls which concerns the possibility of their separate existence in general.

Hence it will be concluded that there can be no rational psychology as Doctrine which procures for us any addition to our self-cognition, but only as Discipline which sets limits to speculative reason, so that materialism is avoided on the one hand, and extreme spiritualism on the other ; and in this manner speculation gives way to practice. Although the position of the immortality of the soul may appear to be injured by these views, which seem to deny that it is impossible to arrive by any

speculative mode at the solution of the question of a
conscious hereafter ; yet it is to be considered that
all such arguments only apply to a dogmatical
system of spiritualism, whilst it leaves the question
itself of immortality untouched, upon such other
grounds, as are furnished by the demands of practical reason, where we may see how many motives
lead us to the conviction that man's existence
is not limited to the earth, but that he is destined
to be a citizen of that higher world, for which he
feels and sees himself formed, but as to which at
present he can form no idea.

The dialectical appearances then in rational
Psychology rest upon an exchange of an idea of
reason, that is of pure intelligence, for the undetermined conception in all points of a thinking
being generally. The unity of consciousness
which lies at the foundation of the categories, is
taken for intuition of the subject as object, and the
category of substance is applied to it, whereas
it is only unity in the thinking—by which alone
no object is given, and to which the category of
substance, as it always presupposes given intuition,
cannot be applied. Hence the subject cannot at
all be cognized.

The subject of the categories therefore cannot,
because it thinks the categories, receive a conception of itself as an object of them, since in order
to think such, it must lay at the foundation its
own pure self-consciousness, which has yet to be
explained. Just in the same manner the subject wherein the representation of time has its
foundation originally, cannot thereby determine its
own existence in time,—and if this last thing cannot take place, then the other view of the subject,

as determination of itself (as thinking being in general) cannot take place, by means of the categories.

The "I think" is, as already implied, an empirical proposition, and contains the proposition " I exist" in itself. But I cannot say; all that thinks exists, for then the property of thinking would make into necessary beings all beings which possess this. And consequently my existence cannot be looked upon as concluded from the proposition " I think," as Des Cartes held, since otherwise the major, " all which thinks exists," must precede, for one is identical with the other. The proposition expresses an undetermined empirical intuition, that is, perception, (therefore it still shows that sensation, which consequently belongs to sensibility already lies at the foundation of this existence-proposition,) but it precedes experience, which is to determine the object of the perception by means of the categories in respect of time ; and yet existence here is no category which has not reference to an undetermined given object, but only to such a one, as that of which we have a conception, and concerning which one wishes to know, if the object is to be placed out of this conception or not. An undetermined perception signifies here only something real that is given, and indeed only as to thinking in general, consequently not as phenomenon—even not as thing in itself, (noumenon,)—but as something which indeed exists, and which in the proposition, " I think," is indicated as such. For it is to be observed, that when the proposition, " I think," has been termed an empirical proposition, it was not meant to say that the I, in this proposition, is an empirical representation,—it is rather purely intellectual, since it belongs to thinking in general. But

without an empirical representation, which affords
the matter for thinking, the act, " I think," would
not take place, and that which is empirical, is only
the condition of the application, or of the use of the
pure intellectual faculty.

In the first edition of the Critick, the author went
into an explanation of these paralogisms much
more completely than in the second. This is
perhaps to be regretted, for the manner in which
the four paralogisms were in the first instance
classed and arranged, contributes greatly to the
clearer explanation of a subject, which is not the
least difficult of the many which the author has
undertaken. The first paralogism is termed that
of Substantiality, and the difference between the
subjective I, and the objective I,—the confounding
of which leads to the paralogism in question, may
thus farther be explained :—" I think my thinking
self," or, I think, I—is the proposition. Now, the "I
think," is the determining self or that consciousness
which accompanies all thinking ; but the second
I, or thought I, is not the same determining self—
but the determined self. The first is not the object that is to be determined, but the second,—
which second is an object given by intuition, and
this I is an object of experience, and it is the I in
the Cartesian sense ; and this belongs not to rational psychology, but to that which is empirical.
The syllogism runs thus : Major :—That whose representation is the absolute subject of our judgments, and consequently cannot be used as determination (predicate) of another thing, is substance.
Minor :—I, as a thinking being, am the absolute
subject of all my possible judgments ; and this I,
or this representation of me, cannot be used as de-

termination or predicate of any other thing. Conclusion :—Therefore I am as thinking Being (soul)
substance.

This reasoning is false in form, and consequently
a paralogism, because in the major, the predicate
has only a subjective reality, whilst in the conclusion, we give to it an objective one ; for if the idea
of I, had an objective reality, it would refer to an
object, and might be the predicate of another
object, but then the I would cease to be absolute
subject or substance. In order that the reasoning
should be just, it would be necessary that the predicate should be the same, both in the major and
the minor, that is, that the conception, substance,
should signify in both cases the logical subject to
which all thoughts refer as predicates. From the
idea of a real substance containing the idea of
invariability, or of a principle of duration, all the
changes of which are only, as it has been stated,
modes, it is impossible to prove the invariability
of the soul, for though the I accompanies all
thoughts, there is no co-relative which can distinguish it from every other object, neither can it be
perceived as an enduring principle, as to which all
thoughts are only changes. It is true that the I, or
the idea of my consciousness as the logical subject,
(which must be always distinguished from the real)
of my thoughts is ever the same, and invariable ;
and in this sense, the I is substance, but then it does
cause us to know, as was before remarked, the I
as object.

The second paralogism concerns the Simplicity
of the soul, and this is stated in the following
terms :—That thing whose action can never be
considered as the concurrence (or empirical effect)

of several acting things is simple. Now the thinking I, or the soul is such a thing as that the action
of it can never be considered as the concurrence of
several acting things,—therefore the thinking I or
soul is simple.

The force of this demonstration consists in the
proposition, that, as several ideas constitute a
thought, they cannot be distributed amongst several
objects, and therefore must be contained in the
absolute unity of the thinking subject. But the
next question then is, how is this proposition itself
proved? Not, certainly, by experience; for this
cannot teach us its necessity, and independently
of this, the idea of absolute unity goes beyond the
bounds of experience. That unity of thought which
consists of many representations is collective, or
such a unity as that whereby the Various is thought
as connected together in a whole; and it may refer
equally as well to that, whereby the substances
which produce the different perceptions are thought
as connected in a whole, as to this, that the thinking subject, really according to its nature, is absolutely simple. Every thought requires the absolute
unity of the subject, yet this is only in order that
we may be able to say, " I think." But this " I
think " is not a real subject or substance, but only
a logical one, and in the proposition before us we
confound and take, as we did in the preceding
one, the unity of ideas as given by the thinking
subject, for objective unity. The proof of the
immortality and incorruptibility of the soul as
based upon this reasoning, falls away with the reasoning itself; for, even in admitting either the simplicity of the soul, or that it is not an extensive
quantity, or one composed of parts, we must still

admit that its consciousness is an intensive quantity, or that it has different degrees of reality in respect to its faculties. But in this case it would be possible, after its separation from the body, that this intensive quantity might diminish until it became zero, not by division, but by the diminution of intensity before explained ; for consciousness itself has such a degree of intensity as may diminish in this way until it loses, as it were, the consciousness of its own consciousness. The substance of the soul, as simple object of external senses, is not and cannot be proved ; nor can the absolute substance of the soul or thinking subject beyond the line of life be demonstrated, which it is the great object of rational psychology to establish, and in regard of which it makes in reasoning, so many valuable but useless efforts.

The third Paralogism is that of Personality, or that syllogism which runs thus,—Whosoever is conscious of the numerical identity of himself in different times (or that he is always one and the same I), is, so far, one person. Now the soul is conscious of the numerical identity of itself in different times. Therefore, the soul is so far one person. In this reasoning the objective substantiality of the soul, and its invariability, are supposed to be proved, and in thus taking the subjective for the objective identity, we fall into the same error as before. For instance, the idea " I think " might be identical, though the thinking subject might be variable. Let us suppose a series of substances, the first of which imparts to others its whole state or consciousness, together with all the representations attached to it,—the second imparts its particular state, also with the state of the preceding substance to the third, and this again its particular state, with both the foregoing to a fourth, and so on. The last substance will therefore be conscious of all the states of the previous changeable substances as well as of its own, because this state, together with the consciousness thereof, was carried over to them, and yet it will not be one and the same person (in itself) in all these states ; so that personality consists in the total synthesis of the determinations of the soul, through apperception, and not in the intuition of the substance, which cannot be proved by personality. Personality does not cease because (through want of consciousness) it is interrupted, and could we even prove the substantiality of the soul, the continuance of consciousness or the possibility of an enduring consciousness in a remaining subject, would not follow ; and this is sufficient as to personality ; for because personality is interrupted for a time, it, as just before stated, does not cease. The impossibility is, to prove that the identity of person follows from the identity of the I of consciousness. There is nothing that grounds one upon the other, and nothing with which to compare the I, in the exchange of representations, except with itself, and this does not amount to any decided proof of personality and substantiality being one and the same thing. On the contrary, it would seem that the latter as permanence is grounded upon the former.

The fourth Paralogism, or that of the identity of external relationship, concerns the reality of the existence of the soul and the doubtful existence of objects, and it runs thus :—That thing as to the existence of which we can only conclude, from its being a cause of given perceptions, can only have a doubtful existence ; or, in other words—Every object whose existence cannot be perceived immediately, and which reasoning alone makes us to be acquainted with, as a cause of given perceptions, has only a doubtful existence. Now all external objects are of that kind that their existence cannot be immediately perceived, but we merely decide upon them as the causes of given perceptions, and consequently, the existence of all external objects is doubtful ; or in another way it may be said, the existence of the soul being the only thing to be perceived immediately, and the existence of all other objects being the result of reasoning, the existence of the soul alone is certain, and the existence of all other objects is doubtful. This doctrine of the uncertainty of the existence of external objects, is the problematical Idealism, before alluded to. Kant, on the contrary, maintains that the objects of the external sense are as certainly existing as the objects of internal sense. This doctrine is termed Dualism, or the theory of the existence of external objects. And it is in order to set aside entirely the doctrine of problematical Idealism that, in the second edition, the author enlarged so much on the point, and greatly changed the form of his reasoning, so as to demonstrate that we have experience and not merely imagination, of the existence of external objects, and that even the internal experience, and which, according to Des Cartes, was alone indubitable, itself was only possible under the presupposition of experience which is external. Now it is true that we can only perceive immediately that which is in us, and that we only know the objects out of us, by reasoning ; but as an effect may have many causes, the effect cannot

enable us to decide upon what may be the determining cause ; and it remains always doubtful
whether the cause of a perception is in us or out of
us. The solution of this paralogism turns upon the
same point as that of the first, inasmuch as it exists
in the distinction belonging to that I which is no
intuition, but which is simple. It accompanies all
our representations, by it we connect the same,
and by it we are conscious that we are the self-
same persons that we were yesterday and the day
previously. This I is pure consciousness (the real
apperception), since it does not come into us by
experience, but first makes experience possible, and
precedes it. But besides this pure I, there is a
changeable I, or an empirical consciousness of ourselves. This is the internal I, wherein is perceived
an unceasing change of our I, and where an unceasing flowing as to the other internal-enduring
simple I, may be perceived. These changes we
perceive or intuify, and in those changeable situa-
tions which we also denominate our empirical I,
partial representations are to be met with—this,
consequently, is intuition.

The critical, formal, or transcendental Idealism
of Kant, is that which explains all phenomena or
sensual objects to be only representations, and not
things in themselves ; or it is that doctrine which
teaches us that whatever is envisaged in space or
in time—and consequently that all objects of possible experience—are nothing but phenomena, that
is, nothing but mere representations, and not things
in themselves ; and that so far as they are represented as extended beings or series of changes,
they have, beyond our thought of them, no self-
grounded existence.

This is the Theory which it is sought to establish as the only one which obviates every difficulty, by showing that space and time are thus mere sensible forms of our intuitions, containing conditions à priori, and under which alone things can be external and internal objects, and which, without such conditions, could be nothing in themselves. Hence the soul is not a thing in itself, but only phenomenon. But by this, it is by no means meant to say that all our consciousness is illusion and goes for nothing, but only, that inasmuch as any doubt with respect to external objects results entirely from our taking what exists in ourselves, as thought, for objects out of us—and the same doubt will exist equally as respects the soul as it does with respect to external objects, if we attempt to establish either as things in themselves, and not simply as results which are entirely the consequence of our individuality—we fall into the difficulties which the elucidation of the Paralogisms as now attempted, can only explain. The I which is the origin of this misunderstanding, may once more be said to resolve itself into four distinct forms.—First, the I, as transcendental self-consciousness, or the fundamental-thought of all thought, or the determining self. This is termed explicitly the psychological fundamental-conception, which contains a certain form of thought, namely, its unity. It is the logical subject of thought, the mere reflecting I, as to which nothing more is to be said than that it is, wholly, simple representation. Secondly, the I as the object of experience, or the object of empirical psychology, and likewise denominated the Soul. It is the I, as empirical consciousness, or the I of the internal sense. It is our internal state, and contains a variety of the determinations which render an internal experience possible. This I is, as to the form, (the mode of representation) but not as to the matter, (the content of it) different from the preceding, that is to say, it is one and the same subject which considers itself as determining and as determined. Thirdly, the I, as object of pure psychology, (which is nothing else but the first I, misunderstood, and taken to be a self-subsisting Being, that can be cognized à priori.) Fourthly, the I, as Noumenon, or transcendental substratum of thought, or the intellectual I—an idea which we lay at the foundation of the quality of our cognition-faculty according to the phenomena of the internal sense. It is a thing in itself (noumenon), as to which consequently we can neither cognize existence nor quality. The distinction between these different views of the I, if well understood, will render the subtlety of the reasoning as to the Paralogisms of pure Reason more intelligible.

The next division of the " Critick," is that which concerns the "Antinomies of Pure Reason." As the first kind of sophistical conclusions refers to the unconditioned unity of the subjective conditions of all representations generally, that is, of the soul, in correspondence with the categorical syllogisms—the second kind of dialectical argument would have for its content, according to analogy with hypothetical syllogisms, the unconditioned unity of the objective conditions in the phenomenon. But in the paralogisms lately under consideration, we remarked only a one-sided appearance, in respect of the subject of our thinking, and that there was not the slightest appearance of probability for the assertion of its contrary, whereas now whilst we are discussing the objective synthesis of phenomena, we shall perceive that there are two sides of the question equally tenable, and yet that both are erroneous.

All transcendental ideas inasmuch as they concern absolute Totality, in the synthesis of phenomena, are termed by Kant cosmical conceptions, partly on account of the unconditioned totality whereupon the conception of the World reposes, which itself is only an idea, and partly because these only refer to the synthesis of phenomena, and consequently to that which is empirical, whilst on the contrary, the absolute totality in the synthesis of the conditions of all possible things in general will occasion an Ideal of pure Reason, which is totally different from the cosmical conception, though it stands in relationship to it. Just, therefore, as the paralogisms of pure reason laid the foundation of a dialectical psychology, so will the antinomy of pure reason expose to view the transcendental principles of a pretended pure and rational cosmology, not in order to find it valid or appropriate in respect of ourselves, but as the name itself denotes, to exhibit the thing as an Idea, whose brilliant and false appearance is not in any way to be reconciled with phenomena.

The function of reason in hypothetical propositions ascends from one supposition to another, until it arrives at the Absolute. The synthesis in this way is regressive. It is progressive when it descends from consequence to consequence until it comes to the Totality. According to the four classes of the categories, the series of subordinate conditions is successively submitted to quantity, quality, relation and modality, and from these

result four cosmological ideas, and as to which,
reason, in endeavouring to apply them to objects,
seeks to establish a rational cosmology. These
four cosmological ideas are divisible into the mathematical and dynamical. The two first are absolute totality in the composition of all phenomena
in space and in time, and absolute totality in the
division of all that is phenomenal, or is in matter.
The two others are absolute totality of the appearance or rise of phenomena, and absolute totality
in the dependence of the existence of the changeable in the phenomenon. Now the Absolute of the
total series may be contained in such a manner
that each member is conditional, and that the whole
only is absolute, or the Absolute itself is a member
of the series, and it is absolutely the first of the
series. These are the only modes in which reason
can look at the Totality of the series of conditions,
and it is these two ways of looking at the Totality
that lead to results quite contrary to one another,
and in fact to the Antinomies which are now under
consideration.*

The first contradiction of transcendental ideas
is seen in the two propositions, that the World has a
beginning in time, and is also enclosed in limits as
to space, and that that world has no beginning, and
no limits in space, but is as well in respect of time,
as of space, infinite. The affirmative and negative
of these propositions being equally provable,

---

* Leibnitz and Wolf maintained that man had as it were two
spheres—one physical, known to him by his senses, the other spi-
ritual, as known to him by his reason. Kant seems occasionally to
fall into this view, but in his Antinomies he came to the conclusion
that there is nothing beyond the limits of experience which is any
guarantee for the correctness of our thoughts.

reason thus falls into contradiction with itself. Yet neither of these antagonist opinions are arbitrary or sophistical, but they are inevitable, inasmuch as reason applies to objects of experience, those principles which do not belong to such a domain, but which in fact only concern the Absolute.

The proof of the thesis that the world has a beginning in time, and is also enclosed in limits in respect of space, is based upon this principle, that if we admit the world has no commencement as to time, any determined time, as, for instance, the present moment, must have been preceded by an infinite time. But the very nature of infinity is that it is never completed, and therefore, if setting out from the present moment we proceed backwards, it will be impossible to find a point where we can stop; and certainly if we do not admit a beginning we can never arrive at the present moment, for in the same way that we can never reach the beginning in starting from the present time, neither can we reach the present moment, in referring only to the infinite: but because we are arrived at the present moment, it must be granted that the world has had a beginning, and consequently, that having such, it is not infinite.

The evidence in favour of the second division of the thesis is derived from the reasoning on the first. For if it were true that the world had no limit as to space, space would then be infinite. But as large space is only distinguishable from small space, because one requires more time to be perceived than the other, it follows, that if space is infinite, the time in which it is perceived must also be infinite, but the one having been disproved, the other falls to the ground as a matter of course.

Having disposed in this way of the thesis, the antithesis comes next to be tested, or that the world has no beginning in time, and no limits in space, but is, in respect of time as well as of space, infinite. This view is supported by the following reasoning.

Let it be supposed that the world has a beginning at any given time, its origin must have been preceded by a time in which it itself did not exist, or was void, wherein nothing would have past, and wherein no one part could have been distinguished from another ; or a time which is free from every event. In a void time no origin of any thing is possible, because no part of such time has in itself prior to another, any distinctive condition of existence, rather than of non-existence. Different series of things may indeed begin in the world, but to suppose the world itself to have had a beginning is an absurdity, and it is therefore, as the antithesis states, infinite. In respect to the second division of the same subject, let us take the contrary, or, that the world, in respect of space, is finite and limited—it finds itself, in this view, in an unlimited void space, and there would therefore exist not only a relationship of things in space, but also of things to space. But as the world is an absolute whole, the relationship of the world to void space, would be a relationship without an object ; and the world is therefore in respect of space, not at all limited, that is to say, it is infinite. For otherwise where is the limit to be placed, since there is only relationship between spaces, so far as they are filled, because we must in some way or other denote these, in order to have an empirical intuition of them.

The observation which arises naturally out of

these different proofs of contradictory doctrines, is
that in one case the world is considered as a quantity, that is, given both with regard to space and
time,—because as the whole time of its existence
is at every instant elapsed, it must be given according to time ; and because in a certain point
of time the whole world is there, it is also given
according to space. But an eternity or infinity of
real states following upon one another can never
have elapsed up to a given (the present) point of
time, (the terms elapsed and infinite, implying
contradiction): and therefore the world must have,
in this view of the question, a beginning. If time
and space are infinitely given quantities, it is not
the same with filled space and filled time, because
something is then given in time and space, that is
to say, objects—the synthesis of which must be immediately determined and can never be thought as
infinite. There is another refutation of this infinity
of the world, with regard to space and time, which
must not be confounded with the preceding ; and
this is the assertion, that as infinity is a quantity beyond which no greater is possible — but
no quantity being the greatest, because every as-
signable quantity can be thought greater—no quantity can be thought infinite, and the world, therefore, cannot be infinite as to space in time. Here
the conception of infinite is that of a maximum,
whilst the true conception of such a quantity is that
of one whose successive synthesis can never be
completed, and the proof of the thesis must show
that the synthesis by which the world is thought as
a given quantity must come to an end. On the
other hand, in favour of the antithesis, it has to be
observed, that its proof rests upon the assertion,

that if the world had a beginning and is bounded
in extent, an empty time must have elapsed before
this beginning of the world, and an empty space
must bound it. Time and Space in this case must
be particular objects and exist of themselves. And
this is not possible, because the lapse of time is only
conceivable by means of change, and space is only
something in relation to the objects which fill it.
Empty space can only be admitted as existing together with the world, because in that case it is
determined by the objects, and is a something, so
far as these are objects. The school of Leibnitz
endeavours to evade this proof of the antithesis by
so changing the conception of the world, that the
conception of boundaries is converted into limits,
but this alters the original idea, which is not allowable, since the thesis only speaks of a *mundus
phænomenon*, and in respect of this and its quantity we cannot by any means make abstraction of
the stated condition of sensibility, without at the
same time annihilating its being. The sensible
world, if it be limited, lies necessarily in the infinite
void. If we do away with this, and consequently
space in general, as condition of this possibility of
phenomena à priori, the whole sensible world then
disappears. But in the problem before us, this
alone is given to us, and a *mundus intelligibilis* is
nothing but the universal conception of a world in
general, in which conception we make abstraction
of all conditions of the intuition of this world, and
in respect of which no synthetic proposition, whether affirmative or negative, is possible.

The second antinomy of pure reason has for its
thesis, that every compound substance in the world
consists of simple parts, and there exists every

where nothing but the simple, or that which is
compounded from it. The proof is based upon this,
that if something exists as complex, and we annul
all conception of it in thought, the simple must
then remain ; because, as no complex part remains
if the simple did not remain, nothing at all would
remain, and consequently no complex substance be
thought. Hence it immediately follows, that the
things of the world are all simple substances ; that
composition is only an external state of them, and
that although we can never fully isolate, and place
the elementary substances out of this state of conjunction, yet reason must think them as the first
subjects of all composition, and consequently, prior
to the same, as simple beings. There is another
way of proving the same thesis, which is, that if
there were not simple substances, each part would
be divisible, *ad infinitum*, and if in thought we did
away with composition, there would be neither
compound nor simple ; and consequently, the existing objects would be a compound or a multiple
of nothing, which is absurd—and thus it again results, that all substances in the world are simple,
and that there is nothing complex, and that though
we may never be able to represent these elementary
substances, reason still will think such.

In looking to such reasoning in favour of the
thesis, care must be taken not to confound the
question of the simplicity of substances with that
of space. The point before us regards only a
Whole composed of substances, that is, a Whole
whose possibility depends upon the parts ; whereas
in space the parts conversely are only possible in
the whole. Space and Time do not consist of
simple parts. If the composition of space is anni-

hilated, nothing remains, not even the points as boundaries; for it is only a *compositum ideale*, not a *compositum reale*, as accidents do not exist of themselves, but are only real so far as they constitute the state of the substance, and so nothing simple remains with regard to them, after having done away with all composition—consequently, nothing at all remains. The previous demonstration rested upon this, that the parts of which the whole is composed are beings existing of themselves; and this does not apply to space, which is itself only something in so far as there are objects given in space; nor to the accidents of the state of substances, which do not exist of themselves. Here the simple is only spoken of as it is necessarily given in the compounded, so far as this compounded can be resolved into its simple, as constituent parts. The proper signification, therefore, of *Monas*, according to Leibnitz's use of the term, ought to refer to that simple which is given as simple substance, as, for example, in self-consciousness, and not as an element of the compounded, which is better termed *Atom*.

The Antithesis to this contradiction has now in its turn to be brought forward; and notwithstanding the apparent clearness of the preceding reasoning, it will be seen that it is equally easy to prove that no compound thing in the world consists of simple parts, and that there exists nowhere anything simple within it.

Every complex substance exists in space. But every space consists again of spaces, and if a substance consists of simple parts, this simple must still fill a space. A part in each space consists of spaces, and that which fills space must consist of as many parts as space itself, and the simple then becomes something consisting of parts. This contradicts itself, and therefore no compound substance can consist of simple parts. Or in another way, it may be said that every sensible object must be able to be envisaged or perceived by intuition; but we cannot have any intuition of a simple object, and consequently a simple substance is only an idea which can have no object corresponding to it in the sensible world—and therefore there is nothing simple in the world. Against the proof of the antithesis which demonstrates the infinite divisibility of matter from the infinite divisibility of space, the Monadists have alleged an unmathematical objection. They maintain that the principle of space being divisible ad infinitum, it is only concluded from arbitrary conceptions, and that it is no longer correct when we speak of the space which matter fills; supporting their assertion upon this, that space is nothing existing of itself,—and only that which determines objects,—and *real* only so far as objects are given, and that it is consequently determined by them; that the abstract composition of pure space does not apply to them, but that, conversely, positions which are derived à priori from the conception of the objects, and independently of their being given in space, must also necessarily apply to the objects in space. But we have only a conception of bodies as phenomena, which the Monadists overlook, and as such space is presupposed. This is the objective condition of the things as objects of intuition, and every thing that applies to space, applies also to these objects; and the question in the antithesis is not to conceive the simple in the conception, of the composed, but to discover in the intuition of the composed that of the simple. If we make abstraction of intuition, we retain merely the conception of an object, or of the necessary unity of consciousness as a mere thing of thought; and with regard to this, the thesis must be correct. For in this conception of an *Ens noumenon*, nothing compound is given, but the composition is arbitrarily thought, and therefore the simple is presupposed. But if the question regards an object of intuition, we must not make abstraction of the condition under which the object is given to us, that is to say, space; and whatever applies to this, must apply to the conditioned also.

The second proposition of the Antithesis goes much farther than the first, which only banishes the simple from the intuition of the compounded, whilst, on the other hand, the second excludes it from all nature. Consequently, this could not be proved from the conception of a given object of external intuition (of the compounded), but from the relationship thereof to a possible experience in general. As therefore something can never be given as an absolutely simple object in any possible experience—and the sensible world must be looked upon as the complex of all possible experience—it follows, that nothing at all simple anywhere is given. The dogmatical assertion against this which undertakes to show by an object of experience, namely by the I, in the representation I think, the absolute simplicity of substance, is defective; for though in the I, we have a representation that contains no variety, which naturally follows from the conception of *thinking*, yet in order to be able to say that this I is a simple substance, the represen-

tation must refer to something permanent in the
intuition. This permanent intuition, however, is
entirely wanting ; and moreover, it is certain that
it can be only thought possible according to the
form of external sense, and consequently as composed, and not as simple.

The third Antinomy declares in its thesis, that
Causality according to the laws of nature is not
the only one from which all the phenomena of the
world can be derived. There is besides a causality
through Liberty (or freedom from nature) necessary to be assumed for the explanation of the same.

If it be assumed that there is no other causality
than from nature, everything which happens presupposes a previous state or cause, of which it is
the consequence. But the causality of a cause is
again something that has happened. It presupposes a still higher cause, whose causality is again
something that has occurred. If, therefore, there
is no other causality than that according to the
laws of nature, then there is no completeness in
the series on the part of causes resulting from one
another. But the law of nature consists in this,
that without a cause sufficiently determined à
priori, nothing happens. Consequently the proposition, that all causality is only possible according
to the laws of nature, contradicts itself in its
unlimited generality ; and such causality cannot
therefore be admitted as the only one—and we are
compelled to admit an unconditioned causality, and
therefore a cause that presupposes no other cause.
In this way, as the conception of cause which
simply begins a series of phenomena is Freedom
or transcendental Liberty, we are compelled to
admit such as the last cause, and without which

cause, even in the course of nature, the successive series of phenomena could never be complete in respect of causes.

The antithesis, on the other hand, asserts, that there is no liberty or freedom in the world, but that everything therein occurs only according to the laws of nature,—because if there were a first cause, the causality of it would be an event which would itself have a beginning.

Every event previously supposes a cause, and consequently, the causality of the first cause previously supposes another cause determining it; which is tantamount to saying, that this first cause is no absolutely first cause, and that therefore there is no liberty in the world. Or, in other words, if there be a liberty or freedom, and consequently a cause whose causality begins a series of events—as every causality is itself a change, since it is the state of the cause in action, which is different from the state of the cause not yet acting—every change, therefore, presupposes a cause and its causality, of which it is the necessary consequence. The causality of freedom or liberty, therefore, also presupposes a cause, and again a causality; but as this contradicts the conception of liberty, its assumption for the explanation of the events of nature is impossible. Hence there is no liberty which, as a supreme cause, begins a series of events, without being impelled to action by a higher cause; but every cause stands under a higher cause. It may be observed with reference to the thesis, that the requirement of reason to appeal, in the series of natural causes, to a first beginning from liberty, is very clearly shown in this, that, with the exception of the Epicurean school, all philosophers of antiquity saw themselves compelled to admit, for the explanation of the motions of the world, a first *Mover*, that is, a Free-acting cause, which began the series of states first and of itself. For from mere nature they did not attempt to render a first beginning comprehensible. And with regard to the antithesis it may also be remarked, that if a transcendental faculty of liberty be conceded for beginning changes in the world, this faculty must be out of the world ; and allowing such faculty of freedom or liberty to a Being, the same can never be an object of experience, but can only be considered as a cause-noumenon, and in this case its adoption makes no difference with regard to the phenomena of nature.

The fourth Antinomy has for its thesis, that something absolutely belongs to the sensible world, which, either as its part or its cause, is an absolutely necessary Being ; and consequently the antithesis runs thus, that there exists nowhere any absolutely necessary Being, neither in the world as its cause, nor out of it as its cause. The antagonist proofs are thus stated.

The sensible world, as the whole of all phenomena, contains at the same time a series of changes. For without this, even the representation of the succession of time as a condition of the possibility of the sensible world would not be given to us.* But every change is subject to its condition, which precedes according to time, and under which condition it is necessary. Now every conditioned that

---

* Time precedes certainly as formal condition of the possibility of changes, objectively, anterior to this ; but subjectively, and in the effectivity of consciousness, this representation is still, as every other, only given by occasion of the perceptions.   ·

is given, in respect of its existence, presupposes a complete series of conditions up to the absolutely-unconditioned, which alone is absolutely necessary. Consequently, something absolutely necessary must exist, provided a change exists as its consequence. But this necessary something, itself belongs to the sensible world. For, granted that it is out of the same, the series of changes in the world would thus derive its beginning from it, without, however, this necessary cause itself belonging to the sensible world. Now this is impossible. For as the beginning of a succession of time can only be determined through that which precedes as to time, so the highest condition of the beginning of a series of changes in the world must exist, when yet this series was not, (for the beginning is an existence before which a time precedes, wherein the thing which begins, yet was not). The causality of the necessary cause of changes, consequently also the cause itself, belongs therefore to a time, consequently to the phenomenon, (wherein the time alone as the form thereof is possible), therefore it cannot be thought, separated from the sensible world as the complex of all phenomena. Hence, there is contained in the world itself something absolutely necessary, (whether this may be the whole cosmical series itself, or a part thereof).

In proof of the Antithesis it is said: Let it be supposed that the world itself is, or that in it there is a necessary being, there would then be in the series of its changes either a beginning which was unconditionally necessary, consequently without cause, which is opposed to the dynamical laws of the determination of all phenomena in time; or the series itself would be without any beginning, and although contingent and conditional in all its parts, yet in the whole absolutely necessary and unconditioned, which contradicts itself, since the existence of a multitude cannot be necessary, if no single part of the same possess necessary existence in itself.

Let it be supposed, on the other hand, that there is an absolutely necessary cause of the world out of the world, then this cause as the highest member in the *series of causes* of changes in the world would first begin the existence of the last and their series.* But still then it must also begin to act, and its causality would belong to time, but precisely by reason of this to the complex of phenomena, that is, to the world, which contradicts the supposition. Consequently, neither in the world nor out of it (but with it in causal conjunction), is there an absolute necessary being.

Now with respect to the Thesis of this fourth Antinomy, in order to prove the existence of a necessary being, I am required, in this case, to use no other than the cosmological argument, which, for instance, rises from the conditioned in the phenomenon to the unconditioned in the conception, so far as we look upon this as the necessary condition of the absolute totality of the series. To seek the proof from the mere idea of a supreme of all beings, belongs to another principle of reason, and such a one must consequently be particularly brought forward.

---

* The expression, to begin, is taken in a double signification. The first is *active* when the cause begins (infit) a series of states as its effect; the second *passive*, when the causality begins (fit) in the cause itself. It is here concluded from the first to the last.

K

Now the pure cosmological proof cannot prove the existence of a necessary being otherwise than as it at the same time leaves undecided whether the same is the world itself, or a thing different from it. For in order to resolve this last, such principles will for this purpose be required as are no longer cosmological, and do not proceed in the series of phenomena—but conceptions of contingent beings in general, (so far as they are considered merely as objects of the understanding,) and a principle for connecting such by means of mere conceptions with a necessary being—all of which belongs to a *transcendent* philosophy, in respect of which this is not yet the place.

But if we once begin the proof cosmologically, in laying at the foundation the series of phenomena and the regressus therein, according to the empirical laws of causality, we cannot then afterwards rid ourselves of it, and proceed to something which does not at all belong to the series as a member. For in the very same sense something must be looked upon as condition, in which the relation of the conditioned to its condition would be taken in the series, which series was to lead to the highest condition in continuous progression. Now, if this relationship be sensible, and belong to the possible empirical use of the understanding, the highest condition or cause can thus only conclude the regressus according to the laws of sensibility, consequently only as belonging to the series of time, and the necessary being must be looked upon as the highest link of the cosmical series.

However, the liberty has been taken of making such a spring (μεταβασις εις ἀλλο γενος). For instance, it has been concluded from the changes in

the world as to the empirical contingency, that is,
the dependence of the same from empirically determined causes; and an ascending series of empirical conditions obtained, which was, in fact,
quite correct. But as they could not meet in this
with a first beginning and no supreme member,
they therefore abandoned suddenly the empirical
conception of contingency, and took the pure category, which then induced a mere intelligible series,
the completeness of which rested upon the existence of an absolutely necessary cause, which now,
as it was bound to no sensible conditions, would
also be freed from the condition of time, for beginning its causality itself. But this proceeding is
quite illegitimate, as we may conclude from what
follows.

Contingent, in the pure sense of the category, is
that whose contradictory opposite is possible. Now
we cannot at all conclude from the empirical contingency as to the intelligible one alluded to. That
which is changed, the contrary of which (of its
state) is at another time real, is, consequently, also
possible; consequently, this is not the contradictory
opposite of the previous state, for which it is required that at the same time in which the previous
state was, the contrary of the same might have
been in place of it, which, from change, cannot be
at all concluded. A body which was in motion
$=a$ comes into rest$=$non a. Now, because an
opposite state from the state a follows upon this, it
cannot hence at all be concluded than the contradictory opposite of a is possible—consequently a
contingent—for it would be required, in respect of
this, that in the same time that the motion existed,
instead of it, rest might have been. Now we know

nothing more, but that rest was real in the following time, consequently also possible.   But motion
at one time, and rest at another time, are not contradictorily opposed to each other.   Consequently
the succession of opposite determinations, that is,
change, does not by any means prove contingency
according to conceptions of the pure understanding,
and, therefore, also, cannot lead to the existence of
a necessary being according to pure understanding-
conceptions.   Change shows only empirical contingency, that is, that the new state of itself, without a cause that belongs to the former state, could
not at all have taken place, agreeably to the law of
causality.   The cause, and provided it is assumed
also as absolutely necessary, must, in this way, still
be met with in time, and belong to the series of
phenomena.

With respect to the antithesis we shall find, if, in
ascending in the series of phenomena, we fancy we
meet with difficulties against the existence of an
absolutely necessary supreme cause, these likewise
must not then be grounded upon mere conceptions
of the necessary existence of a thing in general,
and, consequently, not be ontological ; but must
arise from the causal conjunction with a series of
phenomena, in order to take for the same a condition
which itself is unconditioned—consequently must
be deduced cosmologically and according to empirical laws.   It must, for instance, be obvious, that
the ascending in the series of causes, (in the sensible world,) can never finish in an empirically unconditioned condition, and that the cosmological
argument from the contingency of the states of the
world, according to their changes, occurs contrary
to the admission of a first cause and one absolutely
first commencing a series.

But there is manifested in this antinomy, a singular contrast, namely, that from the same proof whence in the thesis the existence of a primitive being would be concluded, in the antithesis the non-being of the same is shown and with equal acuteness. First, it is said, " *There is a necessary being*," because the whole elapsed time comprises in itself the series of all conditions, and with this likewise, therefore, the unconditioned (necessary). Again, it is said, *There is no necessary being*, precisely on this account, because the whole elapsed time comprises in itself the series of all conditions, (which consequently again are all conditioned). The cause thereof is this. The first argument looks only at the *absolute* totality of the series of conditions, of which one determines the other in time, and acquires thereby an unconditioned and necessary. The second, on the other hand, takes into consideration the *contingency* of all that is determined in the *succession of time*, (since before each thing a time precedes, wherein the condition itself must be determined again as condition), whereby then all that is unconditioned and all absolute necessity entirely disappears. In the meantime the mode of conclusion in both is quite adapted even to ordinary human reason, which frequently falls into the case of being in contradiction with itself, accordingly as it considers its object from two different points of view.

The next question now to be considered is the interest which reason has in these four Antinomies, which are four of its natural and unavoidable problems. The number is precisely four, and cannot be extended or diminished, because there are no more series of synthetic suppositions which limit

the empirical synthesis à priori. In the assertions
of the antithesis we see the principles of pure
Empiricism prevail, whilst in those of the thesis,
Dogmatism is the distinctive sign. On the part of
the latter there is a certain practical interest in which
the right minded participate, for it is essential to
think that the world has had a beginning—that my
thinking self is of a simple and consequently incor-
ruptible nature—that this myself is at the same
time free in its arbitrary actions, and raised above
the compulsion of nature, and finally that the
whole order of things constituting the world, emanates from an original Being,—from whom every
thing else borrows its unity as well as that connexion which it possesses conformable to its end.
These are all so many supports to morality and
religion, which if the opposite view be taken, or
that which the antithesis supposes, we are immediately deprived of. And not only is there a practical interest in the propositions of the thesis, but
also a speculative one. For if we adopt and make
use of transcendental ideas in this manner, we may
embrace entirely à priori the whole chain of conditions, and comprehend the derivation of the conditioned, since we begin from the unconditioned.
This the antithesis does not afford, and it thereby
recommends itself unfavourably, inasmuch as it
can give no answer to the question, with respect to
the conditions of its synthesis which does not leave
interminably always something more to be de-
manded. According to it we must ascend from a
given beginning to a still higher one ; each part
leads to a still smaller part ; every event has always
another event above it as cause, and the conditions
of existence in general rest always again upon

others, without ever obtaining unconditioned main-
tenance and support, in a self-subsisting thing as
original Being.

There is also, what is termed by our author, the
advantage of Popularity, or as it were, general admission of the fact, which does not constitute a
slight recommendation. The common understanding does not find in the ideas of the unconditioned
beginning of all synthesis, the least difficulty, and
moreover it is better accustomed to proceed down-
wards to consequences, than to ascend to principles,
and it has in the conceptions of the First absolute
(as to the possibility of which it does not trouble
itself), a convincing and at the same time a fixed
point, in order thereon to attach a leading string
for its steps. On the contrary, in the perpetual
ascending from conditioned to condition, with one
foot as it were in the air, it meets with no satisfaction.

Now on the part of Empiricism in favour of the
antithesis, there is, firstly, no such practical interest from the pure principles of reason, as morality
and religion carry along with them. Mere empiricism seems rather to take away from both, all
force and influence. If there be no original being
distinct from the world—if the world be without
beginning, and therefore also without author, our
will not free, and the soul of like divisibility and
corruptibility with matter, *moral* ideas and principles thus also lose all their validity, and they fall
together with the *transcendental* ideas which constitute their theoretical support.

But on the other hand, Empiricism offers ad-
vantages in this way that, according to it, the understanding is always limited to its own territory

or the field of experience; and although it carries
its views too far, it limits reason, very properly
when it runs wild, but then it also falls itself into
error, by dogmatising as its own views, and de-
nying more than it can prove.

Each of the two parties, in fact, says more than
he can substantiate, yet in such a way that the
first rouses and encourages knowledge, although
to the disadvantage of what is practical; the second
certainly affords to what is practical, excellent principles, but precisely thereby, allows reason in respect of every thing wherein a speculative knowledge is allowed to us, to indulge in idealistic
explanations of the phenomena of nature, and on
that account to neglect physical investigation.

Yet these important questions are not altogether
insoluble, and though we see that these are conflict-
ing opinions, and that the old dispute between the
Epicureans and Platonists is revived in the Empi-
ricists and the Dogmatists; still in looking to the
matter with attention, it will be discovered that
these questions may be resolved in a certain way;
that is to say, they are such as being founded upon
something higher than experience, are not to be
reasoned upon, as if they were subjected to empirical laws. With all possible perceptions, we ever
remain under *conditions*, confined either in space
or time, and we come to nothing unconditioned,
so as to decide whether an unconditioned is to be
placed in an absolute beginning of the synthesis,
or in an absolute totality of the series without any
beginning. The all in an empirical meaning, is
at all times only comparative. The absolute all
of quantity, (the universe) of division, of derivation,
of the condition of existence in general, together

with all questions, whether it is to be accomplished
by means of a finite or an infinite continuing synthesis, does not regard in any way a possible experience. We should, for instance, not be able, in
the least, to explain better, nor even otherwise, the
phenomena of a body, whether we admit that it
consists of simple or of always absolutely compound
parts, for there can never appear to us any simple
phenomenon, and equally as little likewise, any
infinite composition. Phenomena ask only to be
explained, so far as the conditions of their explanation are given in the perception. But every
thing which may ever be given in them as compounded in an *absolute whole*, is itself no perception. Yet this All, properly, is that, the explanation of which is required in the transcendental
problems of reason.

As, therefore, even the solution of these problems
can never occur in experience, you cannot thus
say, that it is uncertain, what in this respect may
be attributed to the object. For your object is
merely in your brain, and cannot be given out of
the same; you have only, therefore, to provide for
this, to be in accordance with yourself, and to avoid
the amphiboly that makes your idea into a supposed representation of something empirically given,
and, consequently, likewise into an object cognizable
according to the laws of experience. The dogmatical solution is, therefore, not only uncertain, but
impossible. But the critical one which may be
wholly certain, considers the question not at all objectively, but in regard of the foundation, whereupon it is based.

If the object of an idea is then transcendental,
that is to say, when the conception of it implies

that it cannot be given, or is considered as a noumenon, then it cannot be said that it is either possible
or impossible. It only means such an object cannot be thought by the categories, because the objective validity of these only applies to empirical
intuition. With respect to the cosmological ideas
in question, their object is thought as given, though
it is still certain that it never can be given, and the
ground of the illusion lies in the ideas which mis-
lead us and cause us to consider the object of a
conception as given which never can be given, and
we must seek in the idea itself the solution of the
difficulty which arises from its consideration. The
objects of the cosmological ideas are in fact no
objects of experience, though they may be represented to be such, because it is evident that the
empirical synthesis never leads to such objects.
The apparent contradiction does not arise from a
misunderstanding of experience, because in reality
experience has nothing to do with the matter, and
we must apply to reason to solve the supposed error,
and when we apply our common reasoning to things
in themselves as noumena, it is evident that it
must prove erroneous, for such is only based upon
experience and categories, and it at all times only
refers to phenomena.

To prove the falsehood of a certain position, it
sometimes occurs that we admit its truth, and then
show the contradictory consequences which would
thence ensue. This is frequently done in mathematics, and following the same system, if we suppose that the cosmological ideas as given, we shall
then discover that if we consider the unconditioned
of the thesis or antithesis as given, an object will be
too *great* or too *small* for every conception of the

understanding ; and then it is discovered that such an idea is quite void, and without meaning, because as such an idea has only to do with an object of experience, which necessarily is to be adapted to a possible conception of the understanding, it is clear that any thing that cannot be so adopted is as nothing, and this is in truth the case with all the cosmological conceptions, and which on this account involve reason, so long as it depends upon them in ar unavoidable antinomy. For, let it be said, *firstly*, that *the world has no beginning*,—it is then too *great* for your conception, for this, which consists in a successive regressus, can never reach the whole elapsed eternity. Granted, that *it has a beginning*, it is thus again for your conception of the understanding in the necessary empirical regressus *too small*. For since the beginning still always presupposes a time which precedes, it is then, yet not unconditioned ; and the law of the empirical use of the understanding imposes it upon you, to enquire after a still higher condition of time, and the world is, therefore, palpably too small for this law.

It is the same thing in respect of the double answer to the question, as to the magnitude of the world, according to space. For *is this infinite* and unlimited, it is then too *great* for all possible empirical conceptions. Is *it finite* and limited, you ask then, with reason, what determines these limits? Void space is not of itself a subsisting correlative of things, and can be no condition at which you could stop, still much less an empirical condition, that constitutes a part of possible experience. (For who can have an experience of an absolute-void ?) But for the absolute totality of the empirical syn-

thesis, it is at all times required, that the unconditioned is a conception of experience. Consequently a *limited* world is too *small* for your conception.

Secondly, if every phenomenon in space (matter)
consists of *infinitely many parts*, the regressus of
the division is thus always too *great* for your conception, and if the *division* of space is to *cease* in a
member of it, (the simple), it is then too *small* 'for
the idea of the unconditioned. For this member
still always leaves a regressus to further parts contained therein.

Thirdly, if you admit, that in everything which
happens in the world, there is nothing but consequence according to the laws of *nature*, causality of
the cause is thus ever again something that happens, and it renders necessary your regressus to a
still higher cause, consequently the prolongation of
the series of phenomena a *parte priori*, unceasingly.
The mere acting *nature* is hence too *great* for all
your conception, in the synthesis of the events of
the world.

If you suppose events effected *of themselves*, backwards and forwards, consequently generation from
liberty, you then follow up the why, according to
an unavoidable law of nature, and necessitate yourself to go out beyond this point, according to the
causal law of experience, and you find that such
totality of the connection is too *small* for your necessary empirical conception.

Fourthly, if you suppose an *absolutely necessary*
being, (whether the world itself, or something in
the world, or the cause of the world), you thus
place it in a time, infinitely removed from every
given point of time, as otherwise it would be de-

pendent upon another and older existence. But
then this existence is insufficient for your empirical conception, and too *great*, that you ever could
attain thereto through any continued regressus.

But if, according to your opinion, everything
which belongs to the world, (whether conditioned,
or as condition), is *contingent*, then every existence
given to you for your conception is too *small*. For
it compels you still to seek always after another
existence, upon which it depends.

The key to the solution of all this is to be found
in transcendental idealism, which has shown that
the objects of intuition are not things in themselves,
but are only phenomena, and as such perceived in
space and time ; or that they are mere perceptions,
which, so far as they are represented as extended
beings or series of changes, have no existence independently of our thoughts or ideas.

The Realist in idea, on the other hand, forms
from these mere modifications of our sensibility,
things subsisting of themselves, and thence derives
from what are mere representations, idea of things
in themselves. Care must be taken not to confound this our transcendental Idealism with empirical Idealism, which is completely distinct, and
which admitting the proper reality of space, only
considers as doubtful the existence of extended
beings. On the other hand, the critical or transcendental Idealism demonstrates this existence
in spite of it—though if we reflect that if time
and space considered in themselves are no objects,
and have objective reality only in reference to
the objects which are given in them, they are
consequently in themselves nothing more than
the conditions of the intuitions of objects. It

follows that these objects therefore are nothing, if we make abstraction of the intuition, in which they alone are given, and the objects of experience can never be given in themselves, but only in experience, and they do not exist out of the same. If we speak of objects that we have never experienced, as of objects of experience, we then consider them as objects to which the progress of experience or empirical regression may lead ; for when we speak of things that reach out beyond our actual experience, we still think them according to the laws of experience ; for to be any thing as to us, they must be contained in the series of the empirical regressus. If, therefore, we speak of an infinite space—of the whole of elapsed time, &c.— we fall into the consideration of subjects which can never be considered as objects of experience, and which the empirical synthesis can never complete ; and coming to the cosmological idea of an absolute Whole, we consider this to be an object which is given, whilst it is plain that it cannot be given in the intuition, so that we enter upon the consideration of a question which is no longer an object of experience, and then exchange the thing in itself, for one that we assume to belong to experience, treating it in fact as if it were such, when it is not, and cannot in any way belong to it.

The whole Antinomy of Pure Reason rests upon this syllogism—provided that the condition is given, the whole series of all conditions of the same is given.   Now objects of sense are given as conditioned, consequently the whole series of the conditions of these objects is also given.   Through this syllogism then—the major of which appears so

natural and clear—just as many cosmological ideas
are introduced according to the difference of the
conditions (in the synthesis of phenomena) so far
as they constitute a series, as postulate the absolute totality of these series, and precisely by this
means they place reason unavoidably in contradiction with itself.

It is at this step that we come to a right understanding of the points in dispute, and those which
have hitherto appeared so embarrassing. In the
major—we assume that if the conditioned be given
then, the whole series of its conditions is also given,
but it is not possible for us to assume as a given object an infinite series of causes, (which can never be
obtained by the empirical regressus,) and equally as
little is it practicable for us to assume a cause
which presupposes no other cause—and which
other cause must yet be met with in the empirical
synthesis. It thus follows, that in the major which
assumes these, the condition is merely taken in
the conception of the necessary unity, but not as
any thing that is given really, whereas in the minor
the object is thought on the other hand, as an object
of experience—or it may be said, the major of the
cosmological syllogism takes the conditioned in the
transcendental sense of a pure category, whilst the
minor takes it in an empirical sense of a conception
of the understanding, applied to mere phenomena,
that dialectical deception here consequently occurring which is termed *sophisma figuræ dictionis.* Still
this deception is not artificial, but is quite a natural
and consistent illusion of ordinary reason, for if we
make abstraction of a given conditioned in the intuition, and retain nothing in our mind but a con-

ception which pretends to refer to an object, then
it is just as necessary to presuppose the completeness of the conditions as necessary, as it is to do so
with the premises of a syllogism. In the major we
presuppose the conditions and their series, as it were
unseen, when something is given as conditioned,
since this is nothing else but the logical demand to
adopt complete premises for a given conclusion, and
as no order of time is to be met with in the connexion of the conditioned with its condition, they
are presupposed in themselves as given *simultaneously*. Farther, it is equally natural (in the minor)
to look upon phenomena as things in themselves,
and also equally as objects given to the mere understanding, as it occurred in the major, where abstraction was made of all conditions of the intuition
under which alone objects can be given. But we
had then overlooked, in such a case, a remarkable
difference between the conceptions. The synthesis
of the conditioned with its condition, and the whole
series of the latter (in the major) carried along with
it nothing at all of limitation by means of time, and
no conception of succession. On the contrary, the
empirical synthesis, and the series of conditions in
the phenomenon, (which is subsumed in the minor)
is necessarily successive, and only given in time
one after the other ; consequently, we could not here,
(in the minor) the same as there (in the major) presuppose the absolute totality of the synthesis, and
the thereby represented series, since, there, all the
members of the series are given in themselves,
(without condition of time) but here, they are only
possible through the successive regressus ; which
only is given through this, that really we execute
it.

If, as has been shewn, the position, when something is given as conditional an absolute unconditional is also given, be the foundation of this, it is equally evident that such position is not one that can be put, and that the apparently contradictory opposition of Dogmatism and Empiricism is resolved into a nullity. For these assertions are only so far contradictorily opposed one to another as the world is looked upon to be a whole of things in themselves, that is, so far as the categories are considered as absolute predicates; and not that they express the original use of the understanding itself; and when we take, as in the previous series, critical idealism for our guide, we shall find, First, that the world is neither bounded according to space nor time; that it is however just as little infinite, since the world is but an object in the empirical regression, and not independent of it. Secondly, it is equally false to say, that the real in space is compounded of simple parts, as that it consists of an infinite number of parts, since it is but something in the division, i. e. in the empirical regression, and not independent of it. Thirdly, both judgments are false, equally when it is said, that there is a first cause of every series of events, as when it is maintained, that every such series is infinite, since we only understand ourselves in the empirical regression from effect to cause, and have only so far, but not independent of it, object. Fourthly, both judgments, finally, are false, that there is a necessary being belonging to the world, and all existence in connection with the world is contingent; since the conception of world has but an object in the synthesis of understanding and not independent of it.

L

If two mutually contradictory judgments presuppose an inadmissible condition, they both of them actually fall to the ground, when the fallacy is exposed, notwithstanding their opposition, which it must be borne in mind is not contradiction, because the condition falls away under which alone either of the propositions was assumed to be valid.

It follows from the cosmological principle of totality, that no maximum of the series of conditions in a world of sense is given, as a thing in itself, but that it can only be given in the regressus, and that this regressus is only a regulative principle of Reason, which as a rule postulates what is to occur from us in the regressus, but does not anticipate what is given in itself, in the object, before all regressus. On the other hand, the principle of the absolute totality of the series of conditions as given in itself in the object or phenomenon, would be a constitutive cosmological principle, the nullity of which it has been endeavoured to show, and thereby to prevent us from attributing objective reality to an idea which merely serves as a rule. It cannot be stated what the object is, but only how the empirical regressus is to be established, in order to attain to the complete conception of the object.

The distinction between Infinite and Indefinite is of much importance, in the explanation of the cosmological ideas. The regressus is infinite, when that Whole, as to which we are desirous of developing the conditions is given in the intuition. But if only a member of the Series is given from which the regressus is first of all to proceed to the absolute totality, a regressus only takes place indefinitely. The division of matter given, or of a body, proceeds to infinity, because this matter is given wholly and consequently with all its possible parts, in the empirical intuition.

This difference between infinite and indefinite being once understood, it will be easy to see that in the cosmological idea of the totality of the composition of the phenomena of a Universe, that the world as a whole is *not* given in the intuition, either with regard to time or space. The proposition that the I in the empirical regressus always only arrives at a condition which again must be looked at as empirically conditioned, contains the rule in terminis, that is to say, that however far I might reach therewith in the ascending series, I must always enquire after a higher member of the same, whether this be known to me or not by means of experience only. Hence for the solution of the first cosmological principle it will be seen that nothing farther is necessary than to decide, whether in the regressus to the unconditioned magnitude of the whole universe (according to time and space) this never limited ascending-up, may be termed a regression to infinity or in indefinitum. As in this case the cosmological series can be neither greater nor less than the possible empirical regressus upon which alone its conception rests, and as this regressus has given no determined infinite, and also just as little a determined finite (absolutely limited), it is therefore evident that we can neither admit the magnitude of the world, as finite or infinite, inasmuch as the regressus, whereby that magnitude is represented, admits neither of the two.*

---

* This view has been otherwise thus explained. Two theses are said to be in dialectical opposition, that is to say, purely apparent op-

All beginning, it must be remembered, is in time, and all limits of the extended are in space. But space and time are only in the sensible world—consequently phenomena—but limited in a conditional way, but the world itself neither conditioned nor limited in an unconditional way. It is on this account that since the world can never be *wholly given*, and not even the series of conditions for a given conditioned, as cosmical series, the conception of the magnitude of the world is only given through the regressus, and not previous to it, in a collective

position, when the one states in its assertion more than is absolutely necessary to establish the contradiction. Such an opposition admits the possibility of the existence of a medium or intermediate case, which may be true, and by reason of which, both parties are equally wrong. For example, in regard to the two propositions "This paper is white,"—"This paper is black;" neither of the two requires to be true. To establish the contradiction, the simple assertion that the paper is not white, would have been sufficient, and by adding that " the paper is black," we state consequently more than is necessary for the contradiction, and it would require, in the first instance to decide, if the paper may not be yellow, or any other colour, or not exist at all, circumstances by which both parties would be in the wrong. Now this is the case with all the Antinomies, for in the two first we see that both sides look upon the world as a Whole, and they represent this Whole in a particular manner. In stating something with regard to the being or the existence of the world, they say more than is required for the contradiction, and hence it follows that the two Theses are found to be in a dialectical opposition. The medium or intermediate case which here presents itself, and by reason of which both theses are false, is that the World of Phenomena, which, however, only exists relatively to us, does not exist at all, as a Collective Whole, and consequently neither of the parties can be right. The world such as it exists for us is, in respect of phenomena, never a Whole. It is only constantly a part which may become greater as our experience extends farther and farther. In this way this part is never limited, because it may always be extended more and more. But the moment we admit the mere idea of a Whole to be real, and we try to represent this said Whole as finite or infinite, dialectical syllogisms then arise, which the Critick disapproves of, though at the same time, it admits of the impossibility of reason deciding upon the question.

intuition. But the regressus consists always only in the *determining* of the magnitude, and affords therefore no *determined* conception,—consequently also no conception of a magnitude, which is infinite in respect of a certain measure,—consequently, does not proceed to infinity, (as if it were given) but in undetermined extent, in order to give a magnitude (to experience), which first of all becomes real by means of this regressus.

In applying similar general considerations to the second antinomy which we did to the first, and which, likewise, is denominated mathematical; and in following up the same mode of proceeding, we shall find that it is equally as erroneous in this case to say, that the world is either finite or infinite in respect of parts, as it was in the preceding case, to declare that it was so, with regard to time and space. For if I divide a whole, which is given in the intuition, I proceed, in this way, from the conditioned to the conditions of its possibility. The division of parts (subdivisio or decompositio) is a regressus in the series of these conditions, and the absolute totality therefore of this series would only be given, if the regressus could reach to the simple parts. But if all the parts in a continually proceeding decomposition are ever again divisible, the division thus proceeds (that is, the regressus from the conditioned to its condition) in infinitum, since the conditions or parts are contained in the conditioned itself, and as this conditioned itself is wholly given in an intuition enclosed within its limits, they altogether also are therewith given. The regressus is not thus simply in indefinitum—but still it is not allowable to say of such a Whole which is divisible to infinity, that it consists of infinitely many parts. For although all parts are contained in the intuition of the whole, still the whole division is not contained therein, which only consists in the continuing decomposition—nor in the regressus itself which first renders the series real. As this regressus is infinite, so certainly are all the members or parts to which it attains contained in the given whole as aggregate, but not the whole series of the division, which is successively infinite and never entire, and consequently can exhibit no infinite multitude, and no conjunction of the same in a Whole. We see from an investigation of these two antinomies—firstly, that the world has no beginning, with regard to time, nor bounds with regard to space—because otherwise empty time, and empty space, would be real objects, whereas neither time nor space are objects, except so far as something is given in them. There can be no beginning and no bounds to the universe itself, but all beginning and all bounds are only *in* the world, and the objects in the world are therefore limited conditionally, but the world itself neither conditionally nor unconditionally, and for this very reason, the collective intuition of the extent of the universe itself is impossible.

Secondly, we perceive that as we have the body before us, with all its parts we have an empirical Whole, and therefore the regressus in this case is not as in the preceding one, a regressus in indefinitum but a regressus in infinitum, and this constitutes the peculiar difference between the two antinomies. The regression which leads from the conditioned to the condition in dividing the Whole given in the intuition, as for instance the intuition of a body is always accompanied by apprehension because the Whole has in the first instance been given. This does not say that the Body given in the intuition consists of infinitely many parts, because this would imply that the parts were given previous to the synthesis which decomposes the whole in mind, but it simply means, that however far the division is pushed, the empirical consciousness of the parts would still belong to that apprehension, which in the first case apprehended the whole submitted in the intuition, though it might ultimately become so weak as almost to cease to be a real apprehension. The regressus here then, it is evident, 'proceeds to infinity. But then it is only the regressus, and not any thing given prior to the regressus which takes place in the mind. If we were to represent the division of a body as independent of the regression, and all parts as given previous to this, then it would be necessary to represent it as composed of simple parts. For as in a compound substance something real and self-existing is given, the composition belonging only to it accidentally, the permanently given must remain, if even all composition were annihilated ; and as it is no longer compounded it must thus become simple, and the proof of the thesis is correct, if what is given in the intuition be represented as a thing in itself, and its division as independent of the regression. The proof of the antithesis resting solely upon such progression, it concludes quite correctly that the permanent in the intuition does not consist of simple parts, because the object in the intuition is a phenomenon, and not a thing in itself. But in the assertion that the whole consists of infinitely many parts, it falls into the same error as the thesis, inasmuch as it deviates from the empirical regression, and considers the object of the intuition, as a thing in itself.*

As in the first antinomy it cannot be said with truth that the world is a given quantity, and the thesis and antithesis are therefore equally false—inasmuch as the Totality of the world is an idea which we can attain to in experience—only one member however being given to us in intuition, and the others being sought after indefinitely, and not infinitely—the Totality in question is neither more nor less, than the experimental series.   Our senses by which alone we know the world, teach us nothing of infinity ; and in the same way, the world cannot be deemed finite, for in this view, phenomena must be limited by a nothing, or an absolute void, of which we can have no experience, and which, in fact, is an absurdity.   The world as far as we are concerned, is only given by successive perceptions ; and before perception it is not a Whole, and after perception it is not finite, because we seek after its condition.   In the same way the second antinomy

---

* There is however a difference in this rule of progression, if we apply it not to a *quantum discretum* but only to a *quantum continuum*, and the one must not be confounded with the other.   To admit that in each membered or organized Whole, each part is again membered or organized in such a way that in the breaking up of parts to infinity, always new artificial parts are to be met with, cannot be thought, although it certainly may be imagined that the parts of matter in their decomposition to infinity could be membered.   The division of a body in general goes on to the infinite, because the parts themselves are first given in the regressus and not previous to it. This division ad infinitum only concerns the continued quantity, whose parts are not given prior to the decomposition, but the quantum discretum is already given as divided prior to the decomposition, and is in this way distinguished from the quantum continuum whose parts are not given.   The quantum discretum is not therefore membered to infinity, though a quantum may be assumed as being divisible into members, ad infinitum.

rests upon a similar fallacy. No phenomenon can
be looked upon as the smallest, and consequently
none of its parts ; and thus the regressus goes on to
infinity. But this Whole divisible to infinity does
not consist as we have before said of an infinity of
parts given as divided, for the division not being
given before the decomposition in the synthesis,
this consists solely in the regression. This being
infinite, the series of the division is equally so,
and if we follow up the reasoning that matter is
given as an absolute Whole, we shall arrive at the
conclusion that matter is both finite and infinite at
the same time, and this being impossible, it results
that both the thesis and antithesis are erroneous.
This reasoning however applies only to the two
first antinomies, or those which are termed mathematical, but it does not apply to the two latter
or those which are called dynamical, and the cause
of this is plain. In the four antinomies the regression is always from the conditioned to the condition, or it is the hypothetical synthesis, but the
synthesis is very different in the two former and
the two latter antinomies. In the one it is the
synthesis of the homogeneous, in the other the synthesis of the heterogeneous, and though in mathematical connexion of the series of phenomena none
other than a sensible condition can occur, or such a
one as is itself a member of the series, yet on the
contrary, the dynamical series of sensible conditions,
admits an heterogeneous condition which is not a
member of the series, but as intellectual only, lies
out of the series: and in this way the unconditioned
is set before phenomena, without disturbing the series
of such phenomena as are always conditioned, and
thereby breaking it off, contrary to the principles

of the understanding. From the fact therefore that the dynamical ideas allow a condition of phenomena independent, or out of their series, or such a one as is not itself phenomenon, something takes place which is quite different from the antinomy which caused that both dialectical contradictory assertions must be declared to be false. On the contrary, the absolutely - conditioned of the dynamical series, which is inseparable from this as phenomena, connected with the empirically conditioned, yet non-sensible condition, satisfies the understanding on the one hand, and reason on the other, and whilst the dialectical arguments fall away which sought for unconditioned totality in mere phenomena, either in the one or the other manner, the propositions of reason, in the sense now under consideration, may both be true. This can never take place in those cosmological ideas which concern mere mathematical unconditioned unity, because in them no condition of the series of phenomena is met with, but that which is itself phenomenon, and as such constitutes a member of the series. The understanding, we are aware, allows amongst phenomena no condition which should itself be unconditioned. But if an *intelligible* or *intellectual* condition is conceivable, which did not belong to the conditioned in the series of phenomena as a member —yet without completing the series of empirical conditions—such a one might be admitted as empirically conditioned, so that no interruption thereby occurred any where to the empirical - continuing regressus. As the synthesis in the dynamical series is that of the Heterogeneous, it is possible to think the condition of a conditioned given in the intuition, merely by the thought of objective unity, (but this is only problematically) yet being so thought, it may be looked upon—not however as phenomenon, but as thing in itself—and this changes the whole course of reasoning. In the mathematical series we proceed from one empirical space and time to another. There is no determination of the existence of a phenomenon, but only a determination of its place in space and time, and the question according to the synthesis can only refer to phenomena; but in the dynamical series, the existence of a phenomenon is determined. And though the hypothetical series cannot quit the series of phenomena, yet it is permitted to place a thing in itself, problematically, not of that series by which the existence of a phenomenon is determined, though we cannot attain to this by intuition. The antinomy of reason arises when the unconditioned or thing in itself is placed in the series of phenomena. If it be placed without the same, neither the thesis nor antithesis contradict the supposition and both of them admit of being united, as has now to be made manifest in explaining the third antinomy.

It is impossible to conceive more than two kinds of causality in respect of that which happens, that is to say, either one according to the laws of nature, or from liberty. The latter, or as it is otherwise termed freedom, is the power of beginning a state of itself, and the causality of which presupposes no other cause. In this sense it is a pure transcendental idea formed to comprehend the totality of a series of objects in experience, of which the one is the condition of the other, but which totality itself has not been borrowed from, nor whose object can be given in any experience, since every causality thereby given, necessarily presupposes another causality. Now, though this is only a creature of reason, it is necessary to recur to it, if we consider the series of events as given *before* the regression. The antithesis of the antinomy, as it only regards the regression itself, remarks that such regression cannot cease at any member, and hence it denies freedom—but at the same time it falls into the error of making the series of events subordinate to each other as an infinite one, and from the preceding reasoning, it will have been noticed this is only possible by conceiving the same already given *before* the regression. It is especially remarkable that upon the transcendental idea of liberty, the practical conception of the same is founded, and it is particularly the former (the transcendental) which constitutes in the latter (the practical) the degree of difficulty which has at all times surrounded the question of the possibility of liberty. Practical liberty is the independence of the will from necessity, or the impulses of sensibility. It is called a sensual will when it is pathologically affected, and it is called brutal, when it is necessarily determined by pathological notions. But though the human will is a sensitive will, it is not a brutal will, inasmuch as sensibility does not render its actions necessary ; but there is a faculty dwelling in man for the determining of himself, independent of compulsion from sensible impulses only. Now if all causality were mere nature in the sensible world, there could be no practical liberty or freedom, and the doing away with transcendental would at the same time annihilate practical freedom. For this last presupposes, that although nothing has occurred, it might have done so, and the cause in the phenomena was not therefore so determining that a causality did not lie in our own will, independently of, and even against the natural causes alluded to—consequently, a causality for beginning a series of events of itself. But if we investigate this antinomy further, it will be seen that the confusion arises from making the proposition that every event has arisen either from nature or liberty, into a disjunctive proposition, when it in fact is not one, and though it may be deemed extremely subtle to say that an effect in respect of its intelligible cause, may be free, and still at the same time in respect of phenomena as a consequence may be according to the necessity of nature, yet this can be admitted. The general coherence of all phenomena in a context of nature being a continual law, would, if we adhere to the reality of phenomena, overthrow the doctrine of liberty, for if phenomena be things in themselves, liberty is not to be defended upon any ground ; but if they are supposed to be valid for nothing more than they are, that is to say, not for things in themselves, but mere representations cohering according to empirical laws, they then must have grounds, or have a foundation which is not phenomenon ; and such an intelligible cause, together with its causality, is out of the series, but its effects are still found in that of empirical conditions. By adopting liberty as the faculty of a being,—so far as its causality is a thing in itself,—we fall into no antinomy, because we do not contradict the law of nature, or causality, but only determine that it is a rule to which objects of experience are necessarily subjected, and that consequently, so far as an event is an object of experience, the regression in the series of its causes

has no end—but that nevertheless the same event
can be distinctly sought by a causality which does
not presuppose again another causality, so far as
this causality is no object of experience, but a thing
in itself; and the same event may have arisen in
different respects both from nature and from freedom, and the thesis and antithesis may both be
true.

* The possibility of causality through liberty, in
conjunction with the general law of nature, is a
matter which now requires some short explanation.
In the mathematical antinomies we treated of what
was homogeneous, because in speaking of things
connected with time and space and matter, it is
evident that the smallest portion of any of these
was always of the same character as the largest,
and in respect of phenomena, there must necessarily exist between these three things, and the
series of which they make part, a perfect similarity
and homogeneousness.

But in the series of effects and causes,—as to what

---

* If there existed only physical necessity, the imputation of praise
or blame to men for good or evil actions would be wrong, for as no
one by any power of his own could change the nature of a circle
whatever might be commanded, so in the same way would it be impossible to change any thing in our moral conduct, whatever might be
the desire. Duty would under such circumstances be an empty
word, because separated from liberty there would be no option, and
every thing being subjected to immutable laws, all would act from
necessity and be irresponsible. But, in opposition to this we all feel,
that reason dictates to us to perform certain actions, and to abstain
from others, and therefore a power is shewn to act of ourselves, and
this resulting from an inherent spontaneity of our nature. In this
way there is a double character in the actions of men, first as phenomenal, and dependent as such upon physical necessity, and subjected
in this way to the laws of nature; and secondly, as determined by reason only, or an intelligible or intellectual character.

is necessary and what is contingent,—there is nothing which prevents us from supposing that absolute cause and absolute necessity, should not be all phenomena, and that consequently they should differ entirely in their nature from that of the phenomenal part of the series to which they belong. The subject is no doubt beset with difficulty, and to comprehend the same is embarrassing, because however it may be illustrated, it is hard to reconcile the cosmological idea of freedom with the necessity of nature. It is a law of nature that every thing which happens has a cause, but if a free cause were an object of experience, then another causality which had produced this free cause must be enquired into, and freedom as an object of experience would not be freedom. But if we refer the series of events, given in the empirical regression as a whole of phenomena, to a causality out of this series, then we avoid the contradiction ; but then it is also true that we cannot understand the possibility of this causality, which does not stand under the conditions of time. The causality of a Free Cause is certainly not given in experience—neither do we understand the possibility of freedom, nor is its adoption in a cosmological point of view at all serviceable for comprehending the series of events and their totality. But the possibility of the objective reference of such conception we can comprehend, this being only the logical possibility according to which the objective unity of thinking, problematically, is postulated, which is contradistinguished, from the real possibility, wherein an object requires to be thought as given, and the objective unity as given also. Man himself is certainly acted upon by all the circumstances that

surround him, and to this extent he is the creature
of necessity, and if we were able to come at all the
facts which attach to him, we should be able to
know him, as we know any other phenomenon.
But though this be admitted, he always acts under
the consciousness of Liberty, and if he is conscious
of the influence of external objects upon his will
determining him to act, he must also be conscious
of his power to act otherwise, however great that
influence may be. In whatever way a man ac-
knowledges the universal necessity of nature, he
always in his actions must consider himself as
a free being, and admit a consciousness of moral
law. Now this moral law bears the stamp of a
practical position, à priori. He perceives thereby
his intelligible character, or the law according to
which he ought to act, and every action contrary
to that law, he even feels he might have refrained
from. Inasmuch, therefore, as we are conscious
of a power to determine ourselves independently of
sensual motives, and to obey, in opposition to the
same, that practical law, which commands à priori,
we ascribe to reason, a causality ; and this we do
in every thing, which occurs in relation to morality,
although in the action itself, whilst we consider it as
an effect of the causality of reason, there is a sufficient determining motive in the preceding time.
Here we have the double reference on the one
hand to a causality which is itself an event, and
depends upon another causality, and belongs to
a series without end ; and on the other to a causality
of reason itself which is completely grounded in
itself, and by no means presupposes another
cause.

In this view we consider causality as a thing in

itself, and the event itself as an object in the series of intuitions, and in this way the problem is solved, which we had to determine, which was simply to show that liberty did not oppose the necessity of nature in one and the same action, and as in relation to the one, quite another kind of conditions is possible than in respect of the other, the same law does not affect both, and they take place independently of, and undisturbed by, each other.

In the fourth Antinomy, as in the third, we shall find that the thesis and antithesis may both be true; and the solution of the cosmological idea of the totality of the dependence of phenomena in general according to their existence is readily attainable, when we admit that every thing in nature has a conditional and dependent existence, (in which respect the antithesis is true) and yet that there may be an independent and necessary Being, who is the cause of nature. We may admit an intelligible being or noumenon, not belonging to the sensible world, and consequently not subject to the law of causality like phenomena, because it is independent and absolutely necessary. The law of causality is not thereby destroyed, but remains in all its force, as to nature, every member of the series of phenomena being conditional and dependent.

The same series whereby reason ascends to the unconditioned causality, serves also to arrive at an existence that is equally unconditioned. Each member of it, or every causality is again an event, and presupposes another causality. Reason thus forms to itself the cosmological idea of Liberty, in order to comprehend the whole series, and as every member of this series is conditioned with respect to its existence, Reason, which seeks to-

M

tality, creates to itself the idea of an unconditioned existence with a view to comprehend the whole series of conditioned existence.   But the difference between the two last antinomies is important in one respect, and must not be overlooked.   In the third, the object of Liberty, or that to which we attributed the power to begin a series of events of itself, might be an object of intuition, and its causality only must be thought as an object which is not given in the intuition, but in the fourth antinomy, the idea of a necessary Being must be thought as something only intelligible, because it is considered as a substance whose determinations are not subjected to change.   Here the logical possibility of the objective reference of this idea is justified, but the reality of this necessary being is by no means established.

In considering, therefore, the whole of what has been said with reference to the antinomies, which constitute another of the intricacies of the Kantian system, it will be perceived that the two first arise from uniting in one and the same idea two contradictory things, or the phenomenon and the noumenon.   In the thesis and antithesis of the first antinomy, the world is looked upon as a given whole, existing independently of experience, which is equivalent to saying that the sensible world exists out of the sensible world.   The same fault also occurs in the second antinomy.   In supposing that the series of the parts is infinite, the regression from one part to another, never allows the world to be looked upon as a given whole ; whilst in supposing, on the other hand, that it is finite, each part given in the regression is conditional as phenomena, and requires a further division. Thus, in both cases, matter is looked upon as existing independently of experience, when in fact it exists only as phenomenon. The illusion of the two last antinomies arises from reason looking upon that as contradictory which may be united. It is the opposite of what occurs in the two first antinomies.

In the first which are mathematical, we look to magnitude, and it is necessary that the parts should be homogeneous. Every part in the world being phenomenon, the whole world is so likewise. Every part of matter being phenomenal, all matter is equally so. But in the two last antinomies which are dynamical, we only look to the cause of existence, and as this does not suppose that the conditioned is necessarily homogeneous with that which is unconditioned, it may happen that a series of phenomenal conditions may have an heterogeneous cause which is not phenomenon, but a thing in itself, and out of the sensible world. The solution of the fourth antinomy is distinguished from the three others. In it, the solution indicates that the series admitted in the antinomy as totality is not totality, but only a part in experience. The same thing occurs in the third antinomy.

Intelligible causality so far as it has an empirical character, belongs also to the series of phenomena, and it is, on this account, that the ideas of the three first antinomies are called immanent, because they remain within the territory of experience, and may be applied and serve as a rule to it. But in the fourth antinomy the idea of an intelligible Being, and one that is absolutely necessary, must be entirely out of the sensible world, and none of its parts can be found in experience. The accidents in the sensible world are never a whole, but only a part, and whatever may be the magnitude of the series, we never arrive, by its means, at the infinite and absolutely necessary Being, because this Being is not of the series.   On this account the idea of the fourth antinomy is termed transcendent. Thus a gradation is established amongst ideas.   The categories are transcendental but applicable to objects of experience. The cosmological ideas are transcendental when they may be realized in experience.   The idea of an absolutely necessary being is transcendent, it is absolutely ideal ; and having established that independently of what exists in the sensible world, something transcendent may be admitted, and having thus past the confines of experience, we next come to the investigation of the absolutely necessary Being, and seek to derive from our conceptions of this, the conceptions of all things, so far as they are intelligible.   As the consciousness of our freedom in action leads us to the idea of liberty, and to refer it to an intelligible object, so the universal contingency of matter points to the same thing, and man naturally seeks unity as the foundation of what is conditional.

The third division of transcendental Dialectick, and at which we are now arrived, concerns the Ideal of Pure Reason. And as the first division investigated the Paralogisms, and the second the Antinomies, the third will now complete the catalogue, and leave little more of a general nature to be discussed, because the mode in which this Ideal can be conceived is rather an exercise of the imagination than the result of any system which can be laid down. The impossibility of an ontological, cosmological,

or physico-theological proof of the existence of a
God, is shown in the investigation of each of these
theories, and the conclusion at which we arrive,
is, that though transcendental reason allows these
dialectical witnesses to come forward, in favour
of its pretensions, yet, strict attention being paid
to the subject, all this is only found to be that
sort of knowledge, which, inasmuch as it transcends possible experience, man can never attain
to with certainty. All human cognition begins
with intuitions—proceeds thence to conceptions,—
and terminates with ideas ; and although it have
in respect of all the three elements, sources of cognition à priori, which, at the first blush, seem to des-
pise the limits of experience, still having fully considered the reasonings which have been adduced,
it is apparent that all reason, in speculative use,
can never issue out with such elements, beyond
the field of possible experience, and that the proper
determination of this supreme faculty of cognition
is only to avail itself of all methods and principles,
in order to follow up nature into its very core, according to the possible principles of unity, under
which that of ends is the principal—but never to
transcend its limits, out of which there is, as to us,
nothing but void space.

Now with reference to the same immediate subject before us, and which concerns the Ideal in
general, the objectivity of this can neither be af-
firmed nor denied. It is, by its very terms, simply
an Ideal of Pure Reason, but at the same time
supposed to comprehend in itself, as a being, perfect totality of attributes, and to exist in reality.
That such an Ideal can be proved to have any existence is impossible from the proofs that have been

suggested, and which are yet to be taken into consideration, but that the idea itself should arise is very natural, and the mode of its arising is equally so. Practically we seem to have need of such an Ideal as the centre of every thing. To represent mankind in its greatest moral perfection, we must refer to something, as a standard, so that though even objectively we cannot prove its reality, because no intuition can correspond to it, yet it is necessary to reckon upon it for practical purposes. The assumption of a Prototypon Transcendental arises out of the prosyllogism of the disjunctive mode of conclusion, and the principle, that when something is given as conditional, an absolute unconditioned must also be given, is that by which rational Theology seeks to prove the reality of the most real Being. Reason transforms the *distributive* unity of the realities of nature, which are taken from experience, into the *collective* unity of a whole of experience of the sum of their realities. It then hypostatates the unity in placing this collective possibility of all things in one single subject, and this necessitates it even to personify its idea, and to think the most real being at the same time as intelligence—as first principle—and as absolute condition of all possibility.

Three proofs and only three have been furnished by speculative reason as to the existence of God, and all the ways which may be struck out, begin either with determined experience and the thereby acknowledged particular property of our sensible world, and ascend from this according to the laws of causality, to the Highest Being out of the world ; or they lay, simply, undetermined experience, that is, some existence, empirically, at the foundation ;

or they make abstraction finally of all experience, and conclude wholly à priori from mere conceptions, as to the existence of the Highest Cause. These proofs are the physico-theological—the cosmological,—and the ontological. But in examining them in detail it will be observed that reason effects as little in the one way or the empirical, as it does in the other or the transcendental, and that it expands its wings in vain, when by the mere force of speculation it endeavours to rise above the sensible world. The order in which this enquiry will be conducted will be the reverse of that just named, because the ontological will be first taken, then the cosmological, and lastly the physico-theological, inasmuch as though experience furnishes the first occasion for it, it is the transcendental conception merely which guides reason to this its effect, and marks the limit. The investigation therefore commences with the one of the transcendental proof, and then it will be seen what the addition of the empirical can do in augmentation of its force.

First with regard to the ontological proof—proposed by Des Cartes, without which the others have no consistency, but in fact tacitly presuppose it —it must be said, an absolutely necessary Being is that whose non-existence would imply contradiction. Abstraction is made of all experience in this proposition, and the existence is concluded upon only from the idea. Every thing which does not contain a contradiction is held to be possible, and as the idea of a Supreme Being does not imply any contradiction, because being all reality, it excludes all negation and contradiction, its experience is therefore possible. As that which comprehends all reality comprehends also existence, and as the

Ideal of reason does the one, so must it necessarily do the other. This syllogistic form of reasoning may be put in another way, and has been thus laid down. It commences with this major. To whatsoever carries along with it all possible realities or attributes, the reality or attribute of existence must equally belong. Minor. Now the ideal of reason carries along with it all possible realities. Conclusion.—Therefore the reality of existence must necessarily belong to it. This Syllogism also establishes that the simple possibility of the ideal of pure reason carries with it that this ideal exists in reality, and that it would imply contradiction to wish to conceive this ideal as non-existing—and that consequently there exists a Being of an absolute necessity, and whose non-existence would imply contradiction.

But in examining such syllogism attentively we shall soon discover that the major and the minor are not capable of demonstration, the major asserting what requires to be proved, or only saying what is tautological, and from which no proof can be derived. If the assertion, that whatsoever carries along with it all realities, means that every thing which *exists* with all possible realities, &c. the conclusion is then only a useless repetition, for it is obvious that such a thing must have the property of existence, and there is a perfect identity between this and the conclusion, and nothing can be deduced from it. But if this expression mean that amongst the number of the conceivable properties of a thing, the property of existence also belongs, then we are bound to prove that existence may in general be considered in the light of a property or an attribute, for in every thing into which expe-

rience enters, existence has to be presupposed ; and
when it is said that the table is yellow, it is not
stated that the table has the properties of existence
and of yellowness, but on the contrary the property
of existence is found in the conception of table,
before the property of its being yellow is granted.

Whoever would reckon existence amongst the
attributes or possible realities, must consider as
shown the existence of the thing to which he attributes these realities, and yet this was the very
thing first to be proved.   It follows then, that
when we say, the idea of the totality of realities
or possible attributes, carries along with it also the
reality (the attribute) of existence, we do one of
two things—either we attribute existence to the
idea which we erect into an object—with the feeling
that this object does not exist out of our reason,—
or we think that this idea exists in reality out of
us, and that it possesses the properties that we
have comprehended as attached to it.   In the first
case, we do not in any way answer the question
which was to be resolved, except by the ontological
proof which had itself to be resolved, and which
question had for its object to know whether, out of
me, there existed a being of an absolute and perfect
necessity ; and the answer given only concerns, in
one case, a simple idea in me, and in the other, we
presuppose the very question decided which was
at issue, for we admit tacitly that the object to
which we attributed in idea all possible realities,
exists in reality, out of our idea ; and yet this was
precisely the point that had to be proved.

Thus far we have been speaking of the vice,
which manifests itself in the major of the syllogism.
If we go on to the minor we shall see that there is

the same error, and both assume that an idea conceived by us for an object as necessary, exists in
reality out of us as a thing absolutely necessary,
which is the exact position which it was desired
to prove; and though this Ideal may be logically
possible, yet this does not demonstrate in any way
that it is, metaphysically speaking, real and
effective, and that it will agree with the conditions
of experience. The error of the ontological proof is
therefore this. The real possibility of a Supreme
Being is founded upon the logical possibility, two
things which are perfectly distinct; for every
thing that I can think, that is to say, every thing
which is in my conception that does not contradict itself, is not on that account even *really* possible, and if simple possibility be a question, how
much less ought reality or a real existence to be
assigned for it. It is quite certain that it is impossible that a Being which exists necessarily,
should not exist. But how does this advance the
question? The reasoning is simply this, that if
there is a necessary Being, (the very thing which
requires to be proved) it is impossible he should
not exist. The necessity of the existence of this
Being being comprehended in the idea of his existence, one idea carries the other along with it consistently, but does not prove any thing, because
the fact of our conception of a thing does not
prove anything, nor are we at all justified in supposing that because we conceive such, that it really
exists. Finally, the proposition that the Supreme
Being exists really, is either analytical or synthetical. If it be analytical, it supposes that the existence is already comprehended in the subject,
and then the proposition is tautological, and the

judgment that the Being which exists, exists really, is absolutely identical and leads to nothing. If the proposition be analytical, as it ought to be, then it is impossible to demonstrate it, for the only principle of the validity of synthetical judgments is the possibility of experience, and it is evident that experience can furnish no cognition of an object, out of the same, not submitted to sensible conditions. The ontological proof, therefore, of the proposition is impossible.

Nor do we meet with more success in the cosmological proof, which is so denominated, because its minor has for the basis of its support, a phenomenon existing in the world. The reasoning is this : firstly, every object which exists accidentally, cannot be the cause of its own existence. This must be found out of the object. Now that which exists in the world can only exist accidentally. Then that which exists in the world requires a cause out of the same. Secondly, if something exists, it exists necessarily. The I at least exists. Then something exists necessarily. Thirdly, the being whose existence is absolutely necessary is also the most real Being. Now the necessary Being exists necessarily. Therefore it is necessary that he should be the most real. These propositions, besides not being proved, are all based upon the ontological proof which it is wished to avoid. The minor proposition contains an experience, and the major the existence of the necessary Being from an experience in general. The consequence results in this way, and rests upon the pretended natural law of causality—that all which is contingent has its cause, which provided again that it is contingent, must equally as well have a cause, until the

series of causes subordinate one to another, must
terminate in an absolutely necessary cause, within
which this series would have no completeness.   In
fact, the whole of the cosmological demonstration
reposes upon the supposition that an absolute and
necessary Being is also the most real.   This proof,
as we see, begins with experience, but it avails itself
of this support only to make a single step, or one
for the purpose of establishing the existence of an
absolutely necessary Being.   But in order to determine the same with its attributes, experience
can add nothing farther.   It therefore omits experience, and comes at once to the idea, which we
have stated, of the most real Being, and it makes
one of the necessary and most real, but adds nothing
at all to what was before declared to be impossible
as proof.   In regard also as to succession, from effect
to cause in time, this is necessarily, as has already
been shown in the antinomies, phenomenal, and
the principle of causality cannot be applied beyond
the bounds of experience.   The Cosmological idea
cannot elevate the first cause to the rank of the
Supreme Being without Ontology, for every contingent being presupposes a necessary one.   And
the supposition itself has for its basis the conception of causality applied to time, and as time is
only given in experience, it is impossible to found
anything upon this supposition beyond the bounds
of experience, and the conception of causality is
an insurmountable obstacle in the search after a
Being which is subordinate to no other cause.

The error into which the cosmological idea leads
us arises in this way.   It is obvious that contingency is the opposite of necessity, and that the
one cannot be conceived without the other, and

it is equally certain that, in the world, all things
are purely contingent, and that consequently
the thought or conception of phenomena (contin-
gencies) is inseparable from that of necessity.
Now the element of necessity cannot be met with
in the world, all the things belonging to which
are contingent, but as the regulative principle of
reason commands us to conceive and to think
something as necessary, we are then compelled to
place this element of necessity out of the world.
The moment this is done, we convert this said regulative principle into a constituent one, and that
which we have only admitted as necessary, in order
to conceive what is purely accidental or contingent,
we then consider as really something existing, necessarily out of the world, absolutely, and independently. This confusion of the two characters
of reason is natural enough, because, being compelled to admit something which is necessary as
existing, we cannot at the same time conceive it
as non-existing. If by our simple thought or conception, being was really given to the object
thought or conceived, there would be truth in the
syllogistic reasoning upon this subject, but this is
in no way the case, and we therefore, for our own
use, ought to conceive and think something as
existing, without being able to say beyond the
personal use which we make of it, that the thing
itself does exist in reality, and independent of
our thought.

The third proof in favour of the existence of a
God is the physico-theological proof, and this is
the richest in ideas, and the most sublime in its
objects. The present world opens to us so im-
mense a spectacle of diversity. order, fitness, and

beauty, that all language fails us to express the same. Every where we see a chain of effects and causes, ends and means, regularity in beginning and in ending ; and since nothing of itself has come into the state in which it at present is, it always seems to point to something still more remote which renders the same enquiry again farther necessary—so that, in this way, the great Whole would sink into an abyss of nothing, if we did not admit something existing of itself, originally and independently, and external, as it were, to this Infinite-contingent which maintains the same, and as cause of its origin secures also to it duration.

This proof deserves at all times to be mentioned with respect. It is the oldest, the clearest, and the most adapted to ordinary human reason. It animates the study of nature. It manifests ends and views, where our observation had not itself discovered them, and extends our cognitions of nature by means of the clue of a particular unity, whose principle is out of nature. But these cognitions react back again upon their cause—namely, the occasioning idea, and render our belief in a higher Being one of irresistible certainty.

It would, consequently, not only be comfortless, but also quite in vain, says Kant, to wish to take away something from the authority of this proof. Reason, which is unceasingly elevated by means of arguments so powerful, and always increasing under its hands, although they are only empirical, cannot, through any doubts of subtilely deduced speculation, be so pressed down, that it must not be roused, as it were, out of a dream, from any speculative irresolution, through that glance which it casts on the wonders and the majesty of the universe ; in order to raise itself from greatness to greatness, up to the highest of all—from the conditioned to the condition itself—or to the supreme and unconditioned Creator.

But still this physico-theological proof alone can never show the existence of a Supreme Being, but must always leave it, as the cosmological did, to the ontological one to complete the deficiency. The points of this physico-theological proof are these : —1st. In the world, visible signs are found every where of an arrangement executed according to determined intention with great wisdom, and in a whole of indescribable diversity of content as well as of unbounded magnitude of sphere.—2ndly. This fit arrangement is quite extraneous to the things of the world, and adheres to them only contingently, that is, the nature of different things could not of itself, by means of so many means united with one another, accord with determined ends, if they had not been chosen and disposed for this, quite expressly, through a regulating rational principle, according to ideas laid at the foundation.—3rdly. There exists therefore an elevated and wise cause (or more of them), which not merely as a blindly acting all-powerful Nature, through *fruitfulness*, but as an Intelligence, through *liberty*, must be the cause of the world.—4thly. The unity of this cause may be concluded, with certainty, from the unity of the reciprocal relation of the parts of the world, as members of an artificial structure, up to the point where our observation reaches,—and still further, with probability, according to all principles of analogy.

But the proof of fitness and order in the world, however far it was carried, could only demonstrate an Architect of the world, who would always be limited through the fitness of the material he worked upon, but not a Creator of the world, to the idea of which every thing would be subject—but this is very different from what the proof has in view, which was to show an all sufficient First-original. If we would exhibit the contingency of matter itself, recourse must then be had to a transcendental argument, which in this case was precisely what was to be avoided. The advance to absolute totality through the empirical way is quite impossible. But this nevertheless is done in the physico-theological proof. What means do we then make use of, in order to get over so wide a chasm?

After we have attained to the admiration of the greatness, the wisdom, the power, &c. of the author of the world, and can advance no farther, we abandon then at once this argument, conducted upon empirical proofs, and proceed to the contingency of the world, concluded at the very outset from the order and fitness of the same. Now from this contingency alone we proceed, only through transcendental conceptions, to the existence of an absolutely necessary cause, and from the conception of the absolute necessity of the first cause, to the absolutely determined or determining conception of the same—namely, an all-embracing Reality. Therefore the physico-theological proof comes to a standstill in its undertaking—in this embarrassment it springs suddenly to the cosmological proof, and as this is only a disguised ontological proof, it thus completes its intention, really, only by means of pure reason, although in the beginning it had denied all affinity with it, and had placed every thing upon proofs evident from experience.

Hence at the foundation of the physico-theological proof lies the cosmological, and at the foundation of this, the ontological proof, as to the existence of a single original being, as supreme being; and, as besides these three ways, none other is open to speculative reason, the ontological proof from merely pure conceptions of reason is thus the only possible one, provided only, that a proof at all, of a proposition so far elevated above all empirical use of the understanding, be possible.

These constitute the three proofs which speculative reason affords for the existence of the Supreme Being. More cannot exist, and consequently there can be no such thing as rational theology. Speculative reason cannot discover an object corresponding to the logical idea which surpasses all experience, and consequently cannot give reality to it. But though this cannot be proved from speculative reason, it is readily deduced from practical reason, and in a subsequent work upon this subject, forms the basis of a moral system. It is practical reason that leads us to the proof of the existence of God, and with it to the immortality of the soul, neither of which can be proved from the doctrines of theoretic or speculative reason.

God himself being the most elevated of all notions and the reason of all the proofs, he himself cannot be comprehended under the forms of argumentation or demonstration. This was long misunderstood until the time of Kant, who shows in his Critick that all the different proofs of the existence of God as demonstrative forms imply a vicious ratiocination : according to Kant, there is, in respect of the existence of God, only a rational belief, but no certainty. But on the other hand,

N

this rational Theology is of great utility. If it cannot prove the existence of the Supreme Being of itself, it always shows the insufficiency of all those reasonings which are adduced to deny the existence of the same being, the necessity of nature being itself always conditional, and dependent upon a cause which is different from, and is out of the sensible world, for otherwise the existence of the conditional and the dependent, as consequence and effect, would not be comprehensible.

And hence it is seen more undeniably than before, that the ideas of pure reason are not *constitutive*, that is to say, they do not furnish any thing which augments or adds to the sphere of our cognitions, but they are only *regulative* in producing synthetic unity in the same cognitions. They are not ideas of objects, but ideas of the absolute unity of all ideas, which serve as rule to the understanding, and after which unity it naturally seeks—and without which, all our cognitions would be an aggregate, but without harmony or connexion. Transcendental ideas seem as natural to us as the categories, but with this difference, that the last lead us to the truth, that is to the accordance of our conceptions with the object, but the first effect a mere but inevitable appearance ; the illusion of which we can hardly guard against by the strictest Critick, but which it is one of its most important objects to explain and prevent. The transcendental presupposition of unity, which reason seeks to establish, lies concealed in a remarkable manner even in these principles of philosophers ; that all diversities of individual things do not exclude the identity of the *kind*—that the many kinds must be treated only as different determina-

tions of few *genera*, and these of still higher *orders*
—that therefore a certain systematic unity of all
possible empirical conceptions must be sought, so
far as they are to be derived from such as are higher
and more general, in a scholastic rule or in a logical
principle, without which no use of the reason would
take place. For we can only conclude from the
general to the particular, so far as general properties of things are laid at the foundation, and under
which the particular ones stand.

The principle that beings are not multiplied
beyond necessity, or Entia non præter necessitatem,
non esse multiplicanda, and the opposite one that
Entium varietates non esse minuendas, originate
in one and the same principle of the unity of
Reason.*   Both one and the other of these propositions tends to introduce unity into our cognition.
The first sets out from the resemblance which is
visible in the different species of things to ascend
to the highest genera, and the other descends from
the differences existing amongst the different
species to the lower and more individualized differences. These two views may be termed those
of Generalization, and Individualization or Specification. Each acts upon one idea, but the idea in

* Linnæus in furtherance of the first of these principles sought to
reduce nature to a few genera and species, and Buffon, on the contrary, observing the difference of each individual, sought to remove
from Nature, genus and species. The one discovered the unity of
nature in this, that it always acts according to the same plan. The
other maintained that nature always acts according to a different
plan. But both one and the other, the supporter of classification as
well as the supporter of specification, supposed that the principle of
their opposite systems was in nature ; and both agreed in giving an
objective necessity to their idea, whether it was that of homogeneousness or variety.

the one is that of homogeneousness, and the other of heterogeneousness or variety. The principle however which unites both is that of affinity, and the table, so to express it, of the principles of pure reason, is Diversity, Affinity and Unity. Intuition furnishes the Diversity, and the intellect, Unity, and as these two are in contradiction, reason resolves the antinomy by Affinity.

The difference between the terms constitutive and regulative referred to, and upon which most of our Author's reasoning rests, may here still farther be explained. In the transcendental Analytick, it will be remembered that amongst the principles of the understanding, the dynamical were distinguished, as mere regulative principles of the intuition, from the mathematical which are constitutive. The ground of this is, that the mathematical principles justify the understanding in the application of the categories of quantity and quality to the objects of empirical intuition, by which an object is thought as determined, both in matter and form. The dynamical principles, on the contrary, refer to the existence of objects, and are only regulative, because, according to them, that which is the essence of a certain phenomenon is not thought—but only the existence thereof is determined, either in relation to that of another existence, or to the understanding itself. These regulative principles, which in reference to the quantity and quality of phenomena, are only regulative, are again themselves constitutive with regard to existence itself. If we search after the foundation, as we have seen in an earlier part of the work, upon which the understanding supports itself, when it thinks objects by the categories, we find it is the schema of sense, a variety being represented as connected by means of the schema in a necessary unity ; and the principles are constitutive, because they are the rules of the application of these schemata to empirical intuition, and by which application, something is thought as an object in the intuition. The principles of pure Reason, therefore, can never be constitutive, because they cannot be represented in any schema, and such principles require this. But yet it is possible to think them as regulative, though not constitutive; and though for ideas there is no schema of sense possible, there is an analogon of a schema whereby they become determined, though they do not gain thereby any objective reality.

The object to be guarded against is to prevent us from giving an objective value to what is only subjective, and from rendering constitutive what is only regulative, or that simple rule according to which we seek to enlarge our cognition, in order to approach nearer and nearer to the idea itself. It is evident that the transcendental ideas in question do not refer directly or immediately to experience —and by the pure principles of reason no experience becomes possible—but they seem to bring to the forms of unity, as it were, certain cognitions. In this way the Maximum of individualization or generalization is the schema for this particular kind of cognition. The conception of a maximum is not representable in experience, and it is a sort of model or prototype, wherein all that the understanding conceives or thinks is subsumpted as unity, and all cognition arranges itself according to this type; and as the schema is the general model or prototype which adopts itself to all images of sense, it becomes the medium between the sensitive and intellectual faculties. The maximum of the diversity is, as it were, a schema in the case of the transcendental ideas. Except in cosmology, when, as we have before noticed, the ideas of reason fall into antinomies, which place reason in contradiction with itself, we may admit problematically the objective necessity of transcendent ideas, which serve as a foundation to Psycology and Theology, because these ideas are logically possible, inasmuch as they do not imply any contradiction,—but at the same time it must not be overlooked that this is only hypothetical, for there is nothing external to us which corresponds to these ideas.

The idea in fact being absolute or unconditional, it is impossible that any external object can correspond to it, because such object must always be limited and conditional. We do not in this way, we repeat, enlarge our cognition, we only regularize the same. And though we are led to the idea of the supreme Unity by our reasoning, its objective value is not shown. The necessity of this only refers to our cognition, and in this way it is only relative to us—and as it only concerns our own reason, it does not necessarily carry along with it the absolute necessity of a Being, which, as far as we know, has only a relative one, in respect of ourselves and our form of reasoning.

It is only when we forget that this necessity is assumed and we render it absolute, that the admission becomes dangerous—otherwise it is very useful to admit it, for in supposing, for instance, in Psychology an objective relative value as to the I, and in admitting it as a simple and thinking substance, as in the first idea, we put aside all that is

corporeal, and in this way we systematically explain the phenomena of the internal sense, according to laws which seem proper to it. The same
thing occurs in the third idea, when the question is
as to the Supreme Being, for the moment we attach
to this an objective necessity, although this is
merely regulative, and consider the Highest Being
as all powerful and supremely wise and good, our
cognition receives a great increase. We then set
about to look in the world after final intention, and
we dip deeper and deeper by our investigations
into the secrets of nature. But when we cease to
look upon these ideas as regulative, and consider
them as constitutive, we fall into error. The first
fault that springs from this view of the physico-
theological Theist is the fault of slothful reason
(ignava ratio) whereby we consider as perfect that
which is not so, and we lay, at the foundation of
the laws of nature, an Intentionality which is not
true. We continually refer to the idea of a supreme
Being for the explanation of phenomena, without
troubling ourselves with ascertaining whether
nature itself would not suffice for the explanation
of that which we seek, to save labour in an extra-
ordinary cause. The second fault is that of perverse
reason, (perversa ratio). The idea of systematic
unity ought only to serve for this, as a regulative
principle, to seek unity in the conjunction of things
according to general laws of nature, and so far as
something thereof is found in the empirical way,
to believe also that we have approximated to the
completeness of its use, though we shall never
attain to it. Instead of this, we reverse the
matter, and we begin from this point that we lay the
reality of a principle of intentional unity, as hypo-

statical, at the foundation. We determine anthro-pomorphistically, the conception of such a su-preme intelligence—since it in itself is wholly in-describable—and then we press in the ends of nature forcibly and dictatorially, instead of, as we ought to do, seeking them by means of phy-sical enquiry. To take the regulative principle of the systematic unity of nature for a constitu-tive one, and to presuppose hypostatically as cause, that which is only laid, in the idea, at the foun-dation of the uniform use of reason, this is, as it were, merely to confound reason. The inves-tigation of nature takes its course quite alone along the chain of natural causes according to general laws of nature, and certainly agreeably to the reason-idea of a Creator, yet, not in order to derive from such that intentionality in effects which we are always in pursuit of, but to cognize the existence of this Creator itself from that of con-formableness of things to their ends, which is sought after in the essence of the things of nature, and where, it is possible, in the essence of all things—consequently, as absolutely necessary. Now whether we succeed in this last or not, the idea always remains correct, and its use also, pro-vided it have been limited to the conditions of a mere regulative principle.

The question to be answered which results from all this is. First, whether reason compels us, in respect of transcendental Theology, to admit something distinct from the world which contains the ground of the arrangement of the world, and its connexion according to general laws; and the reply to this is—certainly; for, though the foun-dation of individual phenomena can only be discovered in nature by way of experience, yet the foundation of the totality or whole of phenomena is transcendental, and must be placed out of the world. But, secondly, we enquire into the nature of this Being, there, that is to say whether it is Substance, Reality, Necessity, and then it becomes without distinct meaning to us, because as we cannot apply to it empirical properties, and as we are entirely unacquainted with any other, we have no higher means of explanation. If we proceed further and enquire whether we must not at least think this Being, distinct from the world,— then again the reply is, certainly ; but only as object in the idea, and not in the reality, that is to say, only so far as it is an unknown substratum of the systematic unity order and intentionality in the system of the world, which reason must make to itself as the regulative principle of its investigation of nature. We may in fact boldly and plainly admit in this idea certain anthromorphisms which are favourable to the regulative principle, for it is only an idea, which is referred not at all directly to a Being distinct from the world, but to the regulative principle of the systematic unity of the world, and yet only by means of a schema of the same, namely, a Supreme Intelligence who is the Author of this World, according to wise ends. What this first principle of the unity of the world is in itself, is not thereby to be thought, but how we were to employ it, or rather its idea relatively to the systematic use of reason, in respect of things of the world.

TRANSCENDENTAL METHODOLOGY.

HAVING now finished one of the divisions of the Critick of Pure Reason, we arrive at the point when it is necessary to speak of the " Method of Transcendental Philosophy." The " Critick," as we have seen, can have no other materials but those which are furnished by experience, and transcendental Methodology will determine the formal and necessary conditions of these same materials, so as to establish the great system of the work itself. This branch is divided into the Discipline, the Canon, the Architectonick, and the History of Pure Reason.

Now the Discipline of pure reason teaches us, in the first instance, how to avoid giving up ourselves to certain propensities where we have to deviate from prescribed rules, and it is, in fact, that correction by which such propensity is finally eradicated. Discipline in this way is of a negative utility. It hinders us from going astray, but it is not like culture, which is of really positive advantage and assistance, whilst discipline is only corrective. Neither reason applied to experience, nor mathematics stand in need of this discipline. In the one case, experience is required, and in the other, construction, or the fact that the conceptions must be exhibited continually in concreto to the pure intuition, whereby every thing unfounded and arbitrary becomes ostensible. But where neither empirical nor pure intuition hold reason in a visible track, namely, when it is in its transcendental use according to mere conceptions, it then stands in need of so much discipline as may curb its tendency to extension, beyond the narrow limits of experience, and restrain it from extravagance and error, so that in truth the whole philosophy of pure reason is concerned with this negative utility.

Particular errors may be remedied by means of *censure*, and the causes thereof by means of *criticism*. But where, as in pure reason, a whole system of illusions and deceptions is met with, which are thoroughly bound up with one another and are united under common principles, there, quite an especial and certainly negative legislation seems to be requisite, which, under the name of a *Discipline*, from the nature of reason and the objects of its pure use, institutes, as it were, a system of forethought and self-examination, before which no false sophistical appearance can stand, but must betray itself immediately, in spite of all reasons for its justification.

By what is termed the mathematical method, it is expected to procure for philosophy a degree of certainty similar to that which mathematics are in possession of. Now, to destroy this error, it is first necessary to show the difference which exists between the two sciences. Philosophical cognition is the cognition of reason from conceptions; mathematical from the construction of conceptions. To construct a conception is to exhibit à priori the intuition corresponding to it. For the construction of a conception, therefore, a non-empirical intuition is required, which as intuition consequently, is single subject, but which, nevertheless, as construction of a conception (a general representation) must express, in the representation, universal validity for all the intuitions possible which belong to this same conception.

If a man had never perceived a straight line, still by means of construction à priori he will easily receive a representation of the same. Every distance of one object from another will give him this representation, for we cannot see any thing out of ourselves, we cannot perceive, intuitively, objects separate one from the other, without making use for this purpose of the representation and intuition of a straight line. But if a person have never experienced the sensation of sweetness, he will never obtain a representation of the same by the notion that is given of it. Thus we only acquire a representation of qualities or attributes, which is the business of philosophy, posterior to experience, whilst we learn to know, through or by experience, the quantities or magnitudes respecting which mathematics are concerned, posterior to a representation à priori, that is to say, to construction à priori in time and space. In other words, that which is general in the representations in the sphere of Philosophy is abstracted from individual representations, and the individual is itself simply reduced to that which is general. On the contrary, that which is general in the representations in the sphere of mathematics, with respect to the understanding, does not at all differ from what is particular or individual, and it does not require previously to be placed under what is general. If it is wished to know further, whence the difference arises between the two kinds of cognition, to resolve this question it is only necessary to call to mind certain axioms of Transcendental Æsthetick and Analytical Logic. It is not certainly in respect of the analysis of theses and axioms, that mathematics are superior to philosophy. To philosophy precisely it belongs to analyze that which is contained in a conception, and what may be deduced from it, and as this is quite foreign to the business of mathematics, philosophy is in this point not inferior. But mathematics again are much superior to philosophy in respect of synthetical axioms à priori, which they prove undeniably, whilst with regard to synthetic axioms à priori in philosophy, doubts continually are found to arise. We have here to remember that there are two kinds of synthetic axioms, for either the conception of these carries along with it intuition, or it is necessary that this conception has been previously applied to an empirical intuition, in order that by it we may obtain a cognition. In the first case the conception may be constructed, that is to say, the intuition which presents itself simultaneously with the conception, causes that the conception becomes cognition, and with respect to such conceptions, it is natural that the general should be represented simultaneously with the concrete. For the intuition which has once been attached to a conception remains ever inseparable from it. This again is precisely the case with the conceptions of the category of quantity, and with which conceptions mathematics are concerned. But from the moment that a conception, in order that it may be transcendent, and that it is to produce a cognition, has to be applied previously to an empirical intuition, this is not given by the conception, prior to experience, except as a general abstraction, and the concrete cannot be comprehended within it, except when we receive it from experience. This in philosophy is the fate of all synthetical principles à priori.

They do not carry along with them intuition, and they remain, on this account, void of all cognition until they have been attached to some object by experience. Thus therefore, though the two sciences are occupied, as to their content, with conceptions, they are, as to their form, distinguished one from the other. In philosophy we endeavour to derive cognition from conceptions. In mathematics we seek to deduce it from the construction of conceptions. In the latter case, intuition (space and time) is given immediately—in the former, it has to be sought in experience. Nor is the difference between the two branches of science, Philosophy and Mathematics, merely one of form, but they differ in method, and if they are both proceeded with in the same manner, it will be seen that the result is against the former. In mathematics the method is to begin with definitions, to lay down certain axioms, and to prove mediate propositions by certain demonstrations. Now, to define in the mathematical sense, is to represent and produce originally in its limits the complete conception of a thing; or, in the words of the author himself, to define is to exhibit originally the particularized conception of a thing within its limits. It follows from this, that if to define is to represent and to produce originally within its limits the complete conception of a thing, empirical conceptions cannot be defined, for we can never determine whether we have or have not fixed exactly their limits. An empirical conception cannot be in fact defined, it can only be explained. We make use of certain signs to define a thing, but new observations occurring, some of these very signs, which were before employed to define or explain, are done away

with, and others are added ; so that the conception
never stands within sure limits. The same thing
applies to a conception à priori. It cannot be
defined. Substance, Cause, Right, &c. are conceptions à priori, but before defining them, it is necessary to attach them to some objects of experience.
And then it is impossible to know beforehand if
the character which we borrow from experience
will be sufficient to render the conception identical
with the intuition ; and if, in this way, neither empirical nor à priori given conceptions can be defined,
neither can those arbitrarily thought, be so. They
may be explained, but not defined. For, with respect to these conceptions, we are ignorant whether
they are primitive. They have constantly need of
a proof of their internal possibility. It may be
declared, for instance, that it is to be understood
by the word Monster, such or such a thing, and
there may be deduced from it a certain number
of consequences, but then the question is whether,
what it is declared to be a Monster, is possible.
This it would be necessary to prove, and the pretended definition could not be the first of our considerations, nor serve as a basis to the consequences
deduced. It follows from this, that if there is any
thing to which the name of definition rightly
belongs, it can only be strictly those explanations
which are given in mathematics, for in their
quality of conceptions not derived, these explanations are premature ; but in their quality of conceptions, which carry along with them their intuitions, they are complete and detailed ; and in
their quality of conceptions to which intuition à
priori, and nothing that is empirical, serves as a
basis, they represent their objects within its limits.

And if definitions are only suitable and strictly correct when speaking of mathematics, and if philosophy cannot imitate them in this respect, neither can axioms pretend to greater right, in this same territory, but they are as much excluded from philosophy as definitions were, and belong to the field of mathematics, and none other. Axioms are synthetical propositions à priori, so far as they are immediately certain, but a certainty of this kind, which dispenses with all ulterior deduction, is not one which belongs to philosophy. An attribute is joined synthetically to a subject, as, for instance, gravity to a body. When we see a body A, independently of experience, we should not know that it has gravity, or+a, but when we see it fall, we learn by experience, not simply the knowledge of the body A, but of A+a. Now every thesis joins, unites, and attaches, synthetically, an attribute to a subject, but to establish the legitimacy of this, experience is necessary. This occurs in the empirical theses, but, in the analytical theses, it is the analysis of conceptions,—and, in the axioms of mathematics, it is the construction à priori. In the latter, the moment we think the subject, the intuition of which its attribute is composed, is brought back to our mind. For example, with the conception " three points," the intuition is given of the attribute, " plane," and we are authorized to state the axiom that any three points are found in one plane. On the contrary, as the subjects à priori which philosophy treats of, fail in intuition, there exists no reason to affirm of these, and to attach to them, synthetically, any attribute, to the exclusion of every other. On this account we are obliged to have recourse to a deduction, and, from this reason, the principles of philosophy are not of a direct transcendental certainty. Hence also it follows, that philosophy is in possession of principles but not axioms, properly speaking, and though in the Analytick, in the table of the principles of the pure understanding, certain Axioms of Intuition were mentioned, the there adopted principle was itself no axiom, but only served for this, to furnish the principle of the possibility of axioms in general, and was itself only a principle from conceptions. It served to show the possibility of an axiom applicable to intuition.

If then neither Definitions nor Axioms can be applied to philosophy in the same way as to mathematics, neither can Demonstrations, for a demonstration is the showing of an intuition and the apodictical certainty of a thesis. Now the theses of philosophy are either theses of experience, or general theses derived from conceptions à priori. The first are certainly intuitive, but as theses of experience they fail in apodictical certainty. The others may possess apodictical certainty, but inasmuch as they are general, and deduced simply from conceptions, the intuitive quality cannot belong to them. Mathematics only contain demonstrations because they derive their cognition, not from conceptions, but from the construction thereof, that is, from the intuition which can be given à priori corresponding to the conceptions.

Hence it will now be evident that in the speculative application of pure reason, we cannot promise to ourselves the same success from the dogmatic manner of proceeding, as in mathematics. In fact, judgments from conceptions, as the case is in philosophy, are not dogmatical, but only them-

selves arise from the construction of conceptions, as
in mathematics, and it would lead us into error if
we attempted to avail ourselves of such a system
in the speculative use of pure reason, because it
might tempt us to consider as proved that which
in fact was not so.   From this it is rightly pre-
vented by the Critick which so, disciplines us as to
prevent this injurious effect.

Having exposed the advantage of the Discipline
of pure reason in respect of the dogmatical use,
and shown how errors are to be guarded against,
the next point to be considered is that kind of discipline which is to be established, in respect of its
polemical use.   The two parties who deny the proof
of any proposition, one on the ground of ignorance,
and the other upon the principle that both sides
are equally possible, are the Sceptic and the Polemic.
But neither one nor other of these affect the great
questions of Psychology and Theology, that is to say,
there is a future life, and there is a God.   For if reason cannot divine a foundation for such synthetical
assertions, which do not refer to objects of experience, nor their internal possibility, neither will any
man ever prove, by means of pure reason, the contrary, since he must then undertake to show that a
Supreme Being, and the thinking subject in us, as
pure intelligence is impossible; and whence would
he derive that knowledge which would authorize
him to judge synthetically as to things beyond all
possible experience.   In this way there is no Anti-
thectic of Pure Reason, for as Kant expresses it, the
only arena for this would be to be sought after in
the field of pure theology and psychology; but such
ground supports no champion in his full armour,
nor with weapons that are to be dreaded.   He can

only step forth and joke and bravado, which may
be laughed at as child's play. This is a conso-
latory observation, and again gives encourage-
ment to reason—for whereupon would it else rely,
if it, which alone is called upon to dispel all errors,
were itself disturbed, without being able to hope
for peace and quiet possession?

And here the errors of Hume naturally force
themselves into notice, this ingenious philosopher
having by his doubts been one of the main causes
of exciting in the mind of our author those investigations which form the basis of the work now
submitted to analysis. Hume had it perhaps in
thought, though he never fully developed it, that
in judgments of a certain kind we go out beyond
our conception of the object. This kind of judgment, it has been already shown, is synthetical.
How we can go out beyond our conception, and
which we have had, so far, by means of experience,
is a matter of no difficulty to be understood. But we
fancy we are able to proceed further than this, and,
à priori, to go out from our conceptions, and to
extend our cognition. This we attempt through
the pure understanding, in respect of that which
can be an object of experience, or through pure
reason, in respect of the properties of things, or, in
fact, of the existence of such objects as can never
present themselves in experience. Hume did not
distinguish these two kinds of judgments as he
ought to have done, and held this addition of conceptions from themselves, and, as it were, a sort of
self-delivery of our understanding and our reason,
unless impregnated by experience, as impossible,—
and consequently, all pretended principles thereof
à priori, as imaginary; and he supposed that it is

nothing but Habit resulting from experience and its laws, consequently, such as are merely empirical or contingent rules in themselves, to which we attach a pretended necessity. For the support of this he referred to the generally admitted principle of cause and effect. And this most assuredly is certain, that as to the determined effects of causes, or conversely as to the causes whose effects are given, we can only obtain these from experience. But this is not to be confounded with the principle of causality itself. Yet because we can never determine à priori the effects of causes, Hume fancied that the position itself, whatever happens has a cause, to be one of empirical origin, and by no means universally true. He therefore concluded falsely, from the contingency of our determination, according to this law, that the law itself was contingent, and considered its application to objects given to us in experience, just as unwarrantable as its application to objects which can never be given to us.

Thus, in looking at the doctrine of Scepticism, it will be found that it is only as preparatory to a sound Critick of understanding and of reason that it is useful. It is not, and cannot be satisfactive, but it is preparative, and awakens the mind, and causes it to be circumspect and attentive, and to discover that which it is legitimately possessed of.

Now, another part of the Discipline of pure Reason regards the question of its Hypothesis, and, as we have come to the knowledge of this fact by means of the Critick of pure Reason, that we cannot know anything in its pure and speculative use, we may ask whether this does not open so much wider a field to hypothesis, and where we may invent, and opine, if not affirm. But if the imagi-

nation is not to run wild, but only to invent under
the strict superintendence of reason, we shall discover that there must always be previously something wholly certain, and not imagined, or mere
opinion, and this is the Possibility of the object
itself. We cannot for instance suppose any new
original forms, as for instance—an understanding
which should be capable of intuiting its object
without sense—or an attractive power without any
contact—or a new kind of substance, which, as
it were, should be present in space without impenetrability—or presence other than in space, and
duration but in time, &c. In a word, it is only
possible for our reason to make use of the conditions of possible experience, as conditions of the
possibility of things, but by no means independent
of this, to create such ; since the like conceptions,
although free from contradiction, would still nevertheless be without an object. Problematically,
however, it is permitted to us to indulge in hypo-
theses, for the sake of opposing a dogmatical ad-
versary. For as the reasons he may allege with
respect to his views, have no more objective value
than ours, one hypothesis balances the other. For
instance, an answer to the supposed immortality
of the soul is thought by some to be found in the
accidentality of being generated, since it is said,
as it is merely a chance whether a man may or may
not be born, and as this depends, in man as well
as in the irrational animals, upon opportunity, go-
vernment, crime, or other extraneous cause, such
accidentality presents a great difficulty against the
opinion of the duration of a creature extending itself
to eternity, whose life has commenced under circumstances so unimportant, and so wholly left to

personal liberty. But in reply again to this view of the matter it is clear that another hypothesis might be submitted, which would be just as tenable as the preceding one, and thus it might be maintained that the thinking I, in its quality of intelligence, is not procreated, but that it lives from eternity to eternity—consequently the .stumbling-block of the arbitrariness of the procreation of man only bears hard against the phenomenon, man, which without any prejudice to the intelligent principle, may be perishable and dependent upon the will of another; as all *life* is itself of the intellectual character, and is not at all subjected to change of time, and has neither begun by birth, nor will terminate in death.

The Discipline of Pure Reason also applies to proofs and to demonstrations, and it will be seen that relatively to the principles of Pure Reason, which do not belong to the domain of experience, the demonstration must justify why it raises itself above the field of experience, and produces a synthetic union between the subject and the attribute; and to avoid error, which so naturally arises dialectically through syllogisms, we are compelled to adopt certain rules in the demonstrative use of Reason.

The first consists in this, not to seek any transcendental proof, without having previously reflected upon and justified to ourselves, whence we will deduce the principles whereupon we think to establish the same, and with what right we may expect a right issue in the conclusions thence to be deduced. The second particularity in transcendental proof is, that for each transcendental proposition only a single proof is to be found, because each transcendental proposition emanates from one conception and supposes the synthetical condition of the possibility of the object according to this conception. The argument therefore can only be a single one, since besides this conception, there is nothing further whereby the object can be determined, and the proof therefore cannot obtain any thing farther than the determination of an object in general, which likewise is only a single one. The third rule peculiar to pure reason, when in respect of transcendental proofs it is subjected to a discipline, is, that its proof must be never apagogical, that is to say, one derived from the justice of the consequences. For as it is possible that the consequences are not known to us in their whole reality, it might happen that one of them had escaped us, which would destroy the proof. This apagogical kind of proof is distinguished from the ostensive or direct one, inasmuch as the latter is that which, with the conviction of the truth, unites, at the same time, insight into the sources of the same, whilst the former may indeed produce certainty, but not comprehensibleness of the truth, in respect of the connexion with the grounds of its possibility. And hence this is rather an aid than a procedure which satisfies all the views of reason. The apagogical proof is quite correct in mathematical, and is useful in physical sciences, but in transcendental philosophy it is not to be permitted, because, in this it is important to verify, before every thing else, if what we consider as objective is not purely subjective, and from which reason all the consequences may agree. Now, how are we to ascertain that all the consequences which we derive as exact from the hypothesis, are the whole of those

that might suit the object, or that others might
not be presented which would destroy the said hypothesis ? The proof must, as has been just stated,
be direct, if it be essential to establish the truth of
an hypothesis. A direct proof has always this
advantage over the indirect, that it not only leads
to certainty, but exhibits the peculiar source of this
knowledge, namely, that it arises from the principle of the possibility of experience, according to
which we are certain à priori that all the principles of the pure understanding are objectively
valid, because, by means of them alone, the given
in the empirical intuition is thought as an object.

The second part of Transcendental Methodology
contains the Canon of Pure Reason, and by this
is to be understood the complex of principles à
priori of the legitimate use of certain faculties of
cognition in general. Transcendental Analytick
has furnished to us the principles à priori upon
which the correct use of our faculty of cognition
rests, and it has at the same time precisely determined the entire and legitimate extent of its use.
Such science is the canon of the pure understanding. Reason, however, in its speculative use,
contains no principles whose aggregate can be
called a Canon. The chief business of speculative
reason is to be a discipline to itself, in order to
prevent its considering some of its laws as furnish-
ing knowledge, whereas they are only *regulative*
principles for the purpose of giving unity to our
empirical knowledge. If pure reason be only speculative there would be no canon, but, independently of this, there is a practical use of pure reason
which subsists of itself, and has a canon. The
final end of the pure use of our reason is to be found

in the solution to the three questions of the freedom
of the will, the immortality of the soul, and the existence of God.   But in looking to these questions
attentively, we shall find that it is their practical
interest that concerns us, and not the speculative
one, for though we should attain to a knowledge and
understanding of these propositions, we shall find
that when this was accomplished, we have not ad-
vanced far.   Supposing even that we should perceive that the will of man was free, that the soul is
a simple substance, and that we could absolutely
prove the existence of the Highest Intelligence,
we are then obliged to think the first property
only as purely intellectual, and that nothing can
be given in experience, which can be thought by
the conception of causality, which itself has no
beginning.   The perception of Liberty or Freedom
prevents us from following up the series of successively determining grounds as proceeding to the
indefinite, but it does not do more than this;   and
with respect to the Soul as a simple substance, it
can only be regarded by us as noumenon.   If
even the existence of a Highest Intelligence could
be proved, we might unite in a firm point the order
and wisdom discoverable in nature, but this could
only take place in the Universal, or in the conception of the relation of collective nature, (as the aggregate of the objects of intuition) to a merely intellectual substratum, which can never be given.
And all this, as was before stated, is *regulative*
and not *constitutive*.   We are still obliged to explain every event from the laws of nature.   It is
not therefore the speculative interest we have in
these questions that engages us to seek after them
objectively, because we know that no speculative

interest can ever be made of them. The interest we have in them is wholly practical. What is meant by practical is to be understood in the sense of duty ; and here it may be right just to allude to what is really practical in the sense in which the author speaks of practical as opposed to pure reason, and which forms the subject of another very celebrated work. A position with him is practical when it expresses that something is to be done, or rather something ought to be done. There is an *Imperative* attached to it, and all philosophy is, in this way, divided into theoretical or practical. But the practical is what concerns us, as men.

It has been seen, in looking at reason in its speculative use, that we were led through the field of experience into the region of speculative ideas, and that we then fell back again upon experience, so that we investigated thoroughly the various questions connected with it, but yet came to no conclusion that we expected. The great question still left open for enquiry, is whether pure reason may not be met with in the practical use, that is to say, whether such tends to reach the highest objects of pure reason, and whether this kind of reason cannot procure for us, from the point of view of its practical interest, that which has been denied to us wholly in regard to the speculative.

All interest, speculative as well as practical, is united in the three following questions :—" What can I know?" " What ought I to do?" and " What may I hope?" The first question is merely speculative, and we have seen how it is to be answered. The second is practical, and as such it may belong to pure reason, but then it is not transcendental but moral, and consequently it does not concern the particular Critick which has all along been under consideration. The third question, that is to say, provided I do what I ought, what may I then expect, is practical and theoretical at the same time. All our hopes tend to happiness, and though there is undoubtedly a moral law determining à priori (without reference to any empirical motives, or it may be expressed, without reference to happiness) the general demeanor of a man, and at the same time, commanding absolutely, yet reason connects happiness with the fulfilment of this law, consequently this connexion is not objective—for though it cannot be shown, à priori, that happiness will be participated in by him who fulfils the moral law, nevertheless, as the morally disposed are worthy of happiness, if they did not participate in it, the moral law would be a chimæra. The world is called a moral world, and notwithstanding such object is not given, it may be thought as given. It is no object certainly of intellectual intuition, but may be represented as an object of intuition, according to the laws of experience, and though it is only an idea, it is still a practical idea, tending to accomplish this object as much as possible. It is certain that the connexion between happiness and morality cannot be comprehended à priori, but we may hope for it, under the presupposition of a Highest Intelligence, who is looked upon as the author of nature, and as the distributor of happiness, proportionate to the morality of every one. The idea of such an Intelligence is termed, the " Ideal of the Highest Good." God and a Future Life, are two inseparable propositions, if the moral law be any thing at all, or if it is not altogether a delusion.

Reason, in fact, sees itself compelled to accept a wise Author of the world and Ruler, or to look at moral laws as nothing.   Every man regards moral laws as commands, but which they could not be, if they did not connect à priori consequences adequate to them, and if they did not carry along with them, promises and threats.   But this they could not do, if they did not lie in a necessary Being as the Supreme Good, who can alone render such a unity conformable to an end, possible.   This moral theology which we are describing, has this advantage over the speculative, that it postulates the existence of a Supreme Being, sovereignly perfect and reasonable, which could never result from transcendent or speculative theology.   From this Being of Beings, we may alone expect that he has arranged all according to an end—that he *can* do all that he wishes to do—and that he is willing to do all that he ought to do.   Hence Omnipotence, Omniscience, and Eternity.   Hence also we are led à priori to the conception of conformity to ends, and of the órder which is to reign in the physical world—a conception which Physico-theology was obliged to borrow, although imperfectly, from experience. For inasmuch as the Supreme cause of the world is to be endowed with wisdom, it results necessarily that the world is arranged according to certain ends.   We have no other notion of reason except its tendency to conform all its actions to a unity of idea ; and if the universe is the work of a Being, supremely reasonable, he must have created every thing according to one and sole idea, as the supreme and definitive end—and every thing must concur towards such end or objects. Practical reason however having attained this high point, namely, the

conception of a sole Original Being, as the highest
Good, yet must it not in any way presume upon
this, as if it had raised itself above all the empirical
conditions of its application, and reached the immediate knowledge of new objects, so far as to set out
from this conception, and to derive the moral laws
themselves from it. For it is these laws themselves
that lead us to the presupposition of a self-suffi-
cing cause or a wise ruler of the world, in order to
give them effect, and therefore we cannot consider
them again, according to this assumption, as casual,
and derived from a mere will, especially of a will
which we should not have a conception of, did we not
form it agreeably to those laws. So far as practical
reason has the right to lead us, we shall not hold
our actions for obligatory on this account that they
are commands of God, but we shall look at them,
on this account, as the divine commands, because
we are obligated thereto internally. We shall
study liberty, under the unity conformable to its
end, according to the principles of reason, and only
so far believe we act conformably to the divine Will,
as we keep that moral law sacred which reason
teaches from the nature of the actions themselves,
thereby believing we serve this will alone, because
we promote well-being in ourselves and in others.
Ethico-theology is therefore only of immanent use,
namely, to fulfil our destiny here in the world, by
harmonizing with the system of all ends—not fa-
natically, or, in fact, wickedly ever abandoning
the clue of a moral legislative reason in the right
conduct of life, for the purpose of connecting this
immediately with the idea of the Supreme Being,
which procedure would give a transcendental use,
but precisely in the same way as that of mere spe-

culation, would pervert and frustrate the ultimate ends of reason.

Hence the proper way for us to take is not from grace to virtue, but, *vice versa*, from virtue to grace, and it would be an absurd mode of acting, if we were to say, that having obtained a certain and apodictical knowledge of God, we derived the moral law from his will. For this would not only be contradictory, because it is these laws themselves, whose practical necessity requires the presupposition of an all wise ruler of the world, and speculative reason is incapable of leading us to the objective validity of this idea, but it would then destroy the moral principles altogether by explaining such as contingent. For, as it has just been stated, we should then consider the practical laws of Reason as binding, because they are the laws of God, whereas, it is precisely because they are internally binding, that they are considered as his laws.

The final division of the Canon of Pure Reason is made up of an investigation of the different degrees which the human mind possesses, of what is termed the Holding-a-Thing-for-true ; and this is subdivided with the three gradations of Opinion, Belief, and Certainty. Opinion is an insufficient Holding-for-true, subjectively as well as objectively, with consciousness. But if the Holding-for-true is only sufficient, subjectively, and yet is held to be insufficient, objectively, it is then termed Believing. Lastly, the subjectively, as well objectively sufficient holding-for-true is termed Knowledge. The Subjective Sufficiency is named, conviction, (i. e. for myself) but the objective, certainty—(i. e. for everybody).

The kinds of belief, it will be obvious, are varied. There is a necessary belief, or such as cannot be done away with, when no one can discover any other conditions by which the end can be obtained, and the mode of obtaining a Belief is therefore valid for every one, and it is objectively necessary. But if there are various ways of obtaining an end, and we are compelled to adopt some one, this is only subjectively necessary, as for instance, in the case of a physician, who is compelled to do something with his patient who is in danger, but is unacquainted precisely with the disease. His belief in this case is only contingent—another person might perhaps better discover the malady. Such belief as lies at the foundation of the real use of means of certain actions is pragmatical belief. There is also doctrinal belief, which is frequently tested by a wager. Often a man states his propositions with such confident and inflexible defiance, that he seems wholly to have laid aside all apprehension of error. A wager offered startles him. He appears to possess conviction which may be estimated at a pound in value, but not at ten. The first pound he indeed stakes readily, but at ten, he is for the first time aware, which previously he had not remarked, that it is, nevertheless, very possible that he is in error.

The belief in the existence of God may at first be doctrinal belief, for although we are bound so to make use of our reason, for the explanation of the phenomena in the world, as if it were all mere Nature, yet is the unity conformable to its end so indispensable a condition of the application of reason to nature, that we cannot pass it by, particularly as experience offers us abundantly such examples of the same. We know no other condition of this unity of the Highest Intelligence (Being of reason) which has ordered all things according to wise ends. Consequently we must presuppose for our clue, in the investigation of nature (of a contingent design) a wise Creator. The result of our research, also, confirms so frequently the utility of this presupposition, and nothing can be brought against it in a decided manner, that our Holding-for-true is not a mere opinion, but a doctrinal belief in God. In the same way, from the excellence of human nature, and the shortness of life, we arrive at the doctrinal belief of the future existence of the soul. This, however, it must be stated, is only Belief. It cannot be termed Hypothesis, because, in that case, we must be able to connect the order of nature with God, but this is impossible, for the given can only be connected with that which must likewise be considered as given.

Doctrinal Belief must, however, be admitted to have something unsteady about it, and we often cast it away in doubt, though as constantly we return again to it. With moral Belief it is otherwise. For there it is absolutely necessary that something must happen, namely, that we should in all points fulfil the moral law. The object is here indispensably established, and there is only one single condition, according to our view, possible, under which this end coheres with all ends together, and thereby possesses objective validity, namely, that there is a God and a future world. We also know certainly, that no one is acquainted with other conditions that lead to this unity of ends under the moral law. But as the moral precept therefore is at the same time our maxim (as reason then commands that it is to be so), we shall thus infallibly believe the existence of God and a future life, and we are sure, that nothing can render this belief vacillating, since thereby our moral principles themselves would be subverted, which we cannot relinquish without being detestable in our own eyes.

In such a way there still remains to us enough, after the disappointment of all the ambitious views of reason wandering about beyond the limits of experience, as that we have cause to be satisfied with it, in a practical point of view. Certainly, no one is able to boast that he knows there is a God, and that there is a future life, for if he knows this, he is then exactly the man whom we long have sought after. All knowing (if it concern an object of pure reason) can be imparted, and we should likewise therefore be able to hope through such instruction to see our knowledge extended in so wonderful a manner. But no, the conviction is not *logical* but *moral* certitude, and as it reposes upon subjective grounds (moral sentiment), so must we never state, that it is morally certain there is a God, &c., but that we are morally certain. That is, the belief in a God and another world is so interwoven with our moral sentiment, that as little as we incur the danger of losing the first, just so little do we fear, that the second can ever be torn from us.

Thus it will be seen, that moral belief is a matter which is not discernible by philosophy only, but is accessible to every one, and that mankind in general, literate as well as illiterate, high and low, rich and poor, are all subject to its influence. It requires no investigation of science, no research of learning to come to a belief in, or a fear of the truths which ought to guide and regulate humanity. A cognition which concerns equally all men, is, as it ought to be, open to all, and nature, in respect of that which regards all men without distinction, has not to be charged with any partial distribution of gifts ; and the highest philosophy in respect of the essential ends of human nature, cannot advance any further than the guide which this nature has likewise conferred upon the most common human understanding.

Every aggregate of different varieties of knowledge brought as it were, into one focus, according to the idea of the object had in view, is a System. If this be not already traced à priori, but only according to an empirical conception, it is technical but when the object is already traced, that is, in all the parts, and order then can be determined à priori, it is architectonical ; and into this unity of system, what is determinate in cognition, can only enter. Hence the Architectonick of pure reason is the Doctrine which belongs to the system of pure Reason, and as it forms part of Methodology, it must now be treated of.

All cognition flows from two sources, either from what is given, cognitio ex datis, or from principles, cognitio ex principiis. In the first case it is called historical, in the second rational : this last arises either from conceptions, and is then termed Philosophy— or from the construction of conceptions, and is then termed Mathematics.

We possess the former (the historical) when we know so much only as we have received, whether it be from actual experience or the information of others. We possess the latter (the rational) when it is knowledge from principles. Philosophy is the simple idea of a science, which can never be represented in concreto. If we understand by philosophy a system of knowledge, the conception of it is only scholastic and has merely a logical interest; but in a popular sense, it is the science which refers all our knowledge to the essential ends of reason, " Teleologia rationis humanæ," and here the philosopher is not the artificer but the legislator of human reason. Now the essential and the highest end of reason, is the destination of man, and the science of this end is Morality. Metaphysics again divide themselves into the speculative and practical use of pure reason, and are, therefore, either Metaphysics of Nature, or Metaphysics of Morals. The first contain all pure reason-principles from mere conceptions (consequently to the exclusion of mathematics) of the theoretic cognition of all things ; the second the principles which determine and render necessary, à priori, that which is to be done and left undone, (conduct). Philosophy divides itself into two branches, one of which is concerned with the knowledge of what is, the other with the enquiry of what ought to be ; and the former is called speculative philosophy, the other practical : and the principles of philosophy, are either derivable from reason itself, and termed à priori ; or from experience, and termed à posteriori. Reason produces a pure philosophical knowledge, experience an empirical one, and the enquiry how it is possible to acquire philosophical knowledge, is the subject now in hand, or Critick; and when it is a dogmatical treatise, or a system without any examination of the degree of belief it merits, it is, as philosophical system, termed Metaphysick. What in the strictest sense is so termed, consists of Transcendental Philosophy, and the Physiology of Pure Reason. The first concerns

only the understanding and reason itself, in a
system of all conceptions and principles, which
refer to objects in general without assuming that
they were given. This is Ontology. The second
considers nature, that is, the complex or aggregate
of given objects, whether they are given to the senses,
or in any other mode of intuition, and it is therefore
rational Physiology. The use of Reason in this
rational consideration of nature is either physical
or hyperphysical, immanent or transcendent. The
first refers to nature, so far as its cognition can be
applied to experience (in concreto), the second to
that connexion of objects which transcends all experience.

The general idea of metaphysics has disap-
pointed men in its progress, because in the first
instance they expected too much from it. It cannot, it is true, be the basis of religion, but it must
ever, remain as its bulwark, and it always acts
as a restraining power upon human reason, and, by
means of a scientific self-cognition, prevents that
error which speculative reason running wild would
introduce both into religion and morals. Mathematics, and Physics, and even the empirical knowledge of man possess great value as means for the
most part to the contingent, but still, ultimately, the
necessary and essential ends of humanity ; though
only through the medium of a reason-cognition
from mere conceptions, which, however it may be
called, is nothing but metaphysics. Added to which
this last considers reason, according to those elements and highest maxims, which must lie at the
foundation of the possibility of some sciences, and
at the base of the use of all. But if metaphysics
only restrain from error, and do not extend cog-

nition, this does not deteriorate from their value, but rather gives to them dignity and consideration, from the sort of censorial office they assume, which secures the general order, harmony, and, in fact, the well being of the scientific community, and prevents its determined and fertile efforts from deviating from the main point in view, which is the general happiness of mankind.

The last point now to be considered, is that which concerns the History of Pure Reason ; and here little remains to be said but to indicate the different phases under which it has been considered. Men in the infancy of philosophy start from that point where, at a later period of intellectual cultivation, it will be found, they ought rather to have finished, namely, by studying the cognition of God, and the hope, or rather the quality, of another world. Virtuous conduct seems the natural mode of pleasing that invisible power which governs the universe, and hence Theology and Morals are those two main points of reference to which man, in all abstract investigations of reason, has finally devoted himself. It was the first of these which drew by degrees into the consideration of the subject mere speculative reason, and which has since become so celebrated under the general title of Metaphysics.

The changes that have taken place in this subject have been various, but still they all refer themselves to three leading divisions, and are those which consider the object—the origin—and the method. In respect, first, to the *object* of all our cognitions of reason, some were merely sensual, others merely intellectual philosophers. Epicurus was the principal philosopher of the sensual, as

Plato was of the intellectual system. The sensualist school maintained that all reality is in the objects of the senses, and that all the rest is imagination, the intellectual school said, on the contrary, that there is nothing but appearance in the senses, and that the understanding alone cognizes what is true. Secondly, in respect of the *origin* of pure reason-cognitions, the question is whether they are derived from experience, or have their sources independently of it in reason. Aristotle is at the head of the first, or, as they may be termed, the Empirists, and Plato, the chief of the second or the Noologists. Locke and Leibnitz in modern times followed these two great leaders, but there was a degree of inconsistency in Aristotle and in Locke, and especially in the latter. Epicurus was more correct than either, because he never in his conclusions issued out beyond experience, whereas Locke, particularly, after having deduced all conceptions and principles from experience, still maintains that the existence of God, and the Immortality of the Soul, are as evidently to be proved as any mathematical theorem. Thirdly, in respect of *method*, if any thing is to be termed such, it must be a proceeding according to principles; and here the division takes place into the natural and scientific. The naturalist of pure reason, or he (who judges simply according to nature) adopts as his principle that, by means of common reason, more can be effected in respect of the most important problems of metaphysics, than by science. This must be erroneous, for it is evident there are certain means which add to the powers of our nature materially, as for instance, when by the aid of mathematics we discover the magnitude of the moon, &c. The followers of the scientific method are on their part also separated into two divisions, or those who proceed as Dogmatists or Sceptics. Wolf was the type of the one class, as Hume was of the other. In addition to all these systems, there is that critical one which has been developed in the work before us, or " the Critick of Pure Reason," and which differing from all other systems that have preceded it, does, according to the opinion of its Author, explain away the various difficulties which other theories present, whilst at the same time it brings human reason into complete satisfaction with itself, and establishes philosophy upon a sure and intelligible foundation.

FINIS.

C. WHITTINGHAM, TOOKES COURT, CHANCERY LANE.